180 Days of LANGUAGE
for Fifth Grade

during the movie

- ✓ capitalization
- ✓ punctuation
- ✓ parts of speech
- ✓ spelling

Author
Suzanne Barchers, Ed.D.

SHELL EDUCATION

Image Credits

pp. 73 Library of Congress Prints and Photographs Division, LC-USZ62-16225; pp. 87 Library of Congress Prints and Photographs Division, LC-USZ62-68483; pp. 152 Library of Congress, LC-D401-22452; pp. 184 Library of Congress, LC-DIG-cwpbh-03501; pp. 90, 100, 103 Wikimedia Commons; all other images Shutterstock

Standards

© Copyright 2010. National Governors Association Center for Best Practices and Council of Chief State School Officers. All rights reserved.

Shell Education

5301 Oceanus Drive
Huntington Beach, CA 92649-1030
http://www.shelleducation.com

ISBN 978-1-4258-1170-9
© 2015 Shell Education Publishing, Inc.

TABLE OF CONTENTS

Introduction and Research........................... 3

How to Use This Book............................... 5

Standards Correlations 11

Daily Practice Pages 12

Answer Key 192

References Cited.................................. 207

Contents of the Digital Resource CD................ 208

INTRODUCTION AND RESEARCH

People who love the English language often lament the loss of grammar knowledge and the disappearance of systematic grammar instruction. We wince at emails with errors, such as when the noun *advice is* used instead of the verb *advise*. We may set aside a résumé with the incorrect placement of an apostrophe. And some of us pore (not pour) over entertaining punctuation guides such as *Eats, Shoots and Leaves* by Lynne Truss (2003). We chuckle over collections of bloopers such as *Anguished English: An Anthology of Accidental Assaults upon Our Language* by Richard Lederer (1987).

Even though we worry about grammar, our students arrive at school with a complex set of grammar rules in place—albeit affected by the prevailing dialect (Hillocks and Smith 2003, 727). For example, while students may not be able to recite the rule for where to position an adjective, they know intuitively to say *the yellow flower* instead of *the flower yellow*. All this knowledge comes without formal instruction. Further, young people easily shift between articulating or writing traditional patterns of grammar and communicating complete sentences with startling efficiency: IDK (I don't know), and for the ultimate in brevity, K (okay).

So, if students speak fairly well and have already mastered a complex written shorthand, why study grammar? Researchers provide us with three sound reasons:

1. the insights it offers into the way the language works

2. its usefulness in mastering standard forms of English

3. its usefulness in improving composition skills (Hillocks and Smith 1991, 594)

INTRODUCTION AND RESEARCH *(cont.)*

Studying grammar also provides users—teachers, students, and parents—with a common vocabulary to discuss both spoken and written language. The Assembly for the Teaching of English Grammar states, "Grammar is important because it is the language that makes it possible for us to talk about language. Grammar names the types of words and word groups that make up sentences not only in English but in any language. As human beings, we can put sentences together even as children—we all *do* grammar. But to be able to talk about how sentences are built, about the types of words and word groups that make up sentences—that is *knowing about* grammar."

With the publication of the Common Core State Standards, key instructional skills are identified, such as identifying parts of speech, using prepositional phrases, capitalizing, and correctly using commas. Writing conventions such as punctuation serve an important function for the reader—setting off syntactic units and providing intonational cues and semantic information. Capitalization provides the reader with such cues as sentence beginnings and proper nouns (Hodges 1991, 779).

The Need for Practice

To be successful in today's classroom, students must deeply understand both concepts and procedures so that they can discuss and demonstrate their understanding. Demonstrating understanding is a process that must be continually practiced in order for students to be successful. According to Marzano, "practice has always been, and always will be, a necessary ingredient to learning procedural knowledge at a level at which students execute it independently" (2010, 83). Practice is especially important to help students apply their concrete, conceptual understanding of a particular language skill.

Understanding Assessment

In addition to providing opportunities for frequent practice, teachers must be able to assess students' comprehension and word-study skills. This is important so that teachers can adequately address students' misconceptions, build on their current understanding, and challenge them appropriately. Assessment is a long-term process that often involves careful analysis of student responses from a lesson discussion, project, practice sheet, or test. When analyzing the data, it is important for teachers to reflect on how their teaching practices may have influenced students' responses, and to identify those areas where additional instruction may be required. In short, the data gathered from assessments should be used to inform instruction: slow down, speed up, or reteach. This type of assessment is called *formative assessment*.

HOW TO USE THIS BOOK

With *180 Days of Language,* students receive practice with punctuation, identifying parts of speech, capitalization, and spelling. The daily practice will develop students' writing efforts and oral reading skills.

Easy to Use and Standards-Based

These activities reinforce grade-level skills across a variety of language concepts. The questions are provided as a full practice page, making them easy to prepare and implement as part of a classroom morning routine, at the beginning of each language arts lesson, or as homework.

Every practice page provides questions that are tied to a language standard. Students are given opportunities for regular practice in language skills, allowing them to build confidence through these quick standards-based activities.

Question	Language Skill	Common Core State Standard
1–2	punctuation	**Language Standard 5.2**—Demonstrate command of the conventions of standard English capitalization, **punctuation**, and spelling when writing.
3	capitalization	**Language Standard 5.2**—Demonstrate command of the conventions of standard English **capitalization**, punctuation, and spelling when writing.
4–7	parts of speech	**Language Standard 5.1**—Demonstrate command of the conventions of standard English grammar and usage when writing or **speaking**.
8	spelling	**Language Standard 5.2**—Demonstrate command of the conventions of standard English capitalization, punctuation, and **spelling** when writing.

Note: Because articles and possessive pronouns are also adjectives, they are included in the answer key as such. Depending on students' knowledge of this, grade activity sheets accordingly.

HOW TO USE THIS BOOK *(cont.)*

Using the Practice Pages

Practice pages provide instruction and assessment opportunities for each day of the school year. Teachers may wish to prepare packets of weekly practice pages for the classroom or for homework. As outlined on page 5, every question is aligned to a language skill.

Practice pages provide instruction and assessment opportunities for each day of the school year.

Each question ties student practice to a specific language skill.

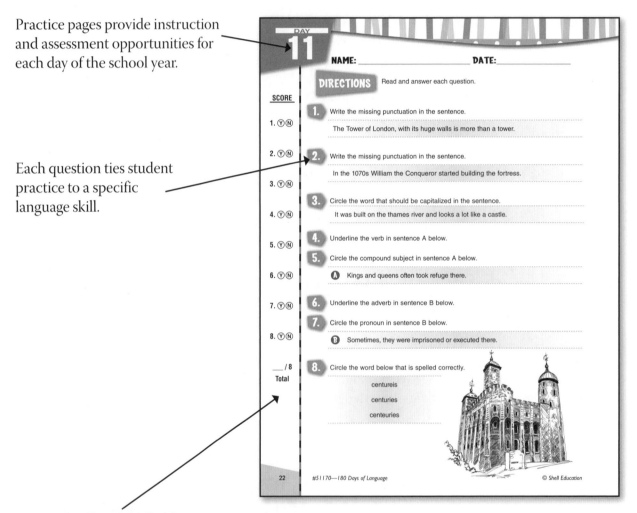

Using the Scoring Guide

Use the scoring guide along the side of each practice page to check answers and see at a glance which skills may need more reinforcement.

Fill in the appropriate circle for each problem to indicate correct (Y) or incorrect (N) responses. You might wish to indicate only incorrect responses to focus on those skills. (For example, if students consistently miss items 2 and 4, they may need additional help with those concepts as outlined in the table on page 5.) Use the answer key at the back of the book to score the problems, or you may call out answers to have students self-score or peer-score their work.

HOW TO USE THIS BOOK *(cont.)*

Diagnostic Assessment

Teachers can use the practice pages as diagnostic assessments. The data-analysis tools included with the book enable teachers or parents to quickly score students' work and monitor their progress. Teachers and parents can see at a glance which language skills students may need to target in order to develop proficiency.

After students complete a practice page, grade each page using the answer key (pages 192–206). Then, complete the *Practice Page Item Analysis* for the appropriate day (page 8) for the whole class or the *Student Item Analysis* (page 9) for individual students. These charts are also provided on the Digital Resource CD as PDFs, Microsoft Word® files, and as Microsoft Excel® files (filenames: pageitem.pdf, pageitem.doc, pageitem.xls; studentitem.pdf, studentitem.doc, studentitem.xls). Teachers can input data into the electronic files directly on the computer, or they can print the pages and analyze students' work using paper and pencil.

To complete the Practice Page Item Analyses:

* Write or type students' names in the far-left column. Depending on the number of students, more than one copy of the form may be needed, or you may need to add rows.

* The item numbers are included across the top of the chart. Each item correlates with the matching question number from the practice page.

* For each student, record an *X* in the column if the student has the item incorrect. If the item is correct, leave the space in the column blank.

* If you are using the Excel file, totals will be automatically generated. If you are using the Word file or if you have printed the PDF, you will need to compute the totals. Count the *X*s in each row and column and fill in the correct boxes.

To complete the Student Item Analyses:

* Write or type the student's name on the top row. This form tracks the ongoing progress of each student, so one copy per student is necessary.

* The item numbers are included across the top of the chart. Each item correlates with the matching question number from the practice page.

* For each day, record an *X* in the column if the student has the item incorrect. If the item is correct, leave the item blank.

* If you are using the Excel file, totals will be automatically generated. If you are using the Word file or if you have printed the PDF, you will need to compute the totals. Count the *X*s in each row and column and fill in the correct boxes.

HOW TO USE THIS BOOK (cont.)

Practice Page Item Analysis

Directions: Record an X in cells to indicate where students have missed questions. Add up the totals. You can view: (1) which questions/concepts were missed per student; (2) the total correct score for each student; and (3) the total number of students who missed each question.

Day: _____ Student Name	Question # 1	2	3	4	5	6	7	8	# correct
Sample Student		x			x	x			5/8
# of students missing each question									

HOW TO USE THIS BOOK *(cont.)*

Student Item Analysis

Directions: Record an *X* in cells to indicate where the student has missed questions. Add up the totals. You can view: (1) which questions/concepts the student missed; (2) the total correct score per day; and (3) the total number of times each question/concept was missed.

Student Name: **Sample Student**									
Question	**1**	**2**	**3**	**4**	**5**	**6**	**7**	**8**	**# correct**
Day									
1		X		X	X		X		4/8
Total									

HOW TO USE THIS BOOK *(cont.)*

Using the Results to Differentiate Instruction

Once results are gathered and analyzed, teachers can use the results to inform the way they differentiate instruction. The data can help determine which concepts are the most difficult for students and which need additional instructional support and continued practice. Depending on how often the practice pages are scored, results can be considered for instructional support on a daily or weekly basis.

Whole-Class Support

The results of the diagnostic analysis may show that the entire class is struggling with a particular concept or group of concepts. If these concepts have been taught in the past, this indicates that further instruction or reteaching is necessary. If these concepts have not been taught in the past, this data is a great preassessment and may demonstrate that students do not have a working knowledge of the concepts. Thus, careful planning for the length of the unit(s) or lesson(s) must be considered, and additional front-loading may be required.

Small-Group or Individual Support

The results of the diagnostic analysis may show that an individual or a small group of students is struggling with a particular concept or group of concepts. If these concepts have been taught in the past, this indicates that further instruction or reteaching is necessary. Consider pulling aside these students while others are working independently to instruct further on the concept(s). Teachers can also use the results to help identify individuals or groups of proficient students who are ready for enrichment or above-grade-level instruction. These students may benefit from independent learning contracts or more challenging activities. Students may also benefit from extra practice using games or computer-based resources.

Digital Resource CD

The Digital Resource CD provides the following resources:

- Standards Correlations Chart

- reproducible PDFs of each practice page

- directions for completing the diagnostic Item Analysis forms

- *Practice Page Item Analysis* PDFs, Word documents, and Excel spreadsheets

- *Student Item Analysis* PDFs, Word documents, and Excel spreadsheets

STANDARDS CORRELATIONS

Shell Education is committed to producing educational materials that are research and standards based. In this effort, we have correlated all of our products to the academic standards of all 50 states, the District of Columbia, the Department of Defense Dependents Schools, and all Canadian provinces.

How to Find Standards Correlations

To print a customized correlation report of this product for your state, visit our website at http://www.shelleducation.com and follow the on-screen directions. If you require assistance in printing correlation reports, please contact our Customer Service Department at 1-877-777-3450.

Purpose and Intent of Standards

Legislation mandates that all states adopt academic standards that identify the skills students will learn in kindergarten through grade twelve. Many states also have standards for Pre–K. This same legislation sets requirements to ensure the standards are detailed and comprehensive.

Standards are designed to focus instruction and guide adoption of curricula. Standards are statements that describe the criteria necessary for students to meet specific academic goals. They define the knowledge, skills, and content students should acquire at each level. Standards are also used to develop standardized tests to evaluate students' academic progress. Teachers are required to demonstrate how their lessons meet state standards. State standards are used in the development of all of our products, so educators can be assured they meet the academic requirements of each state.

Common Core State Standards

The activities in this book are aligned to the Common Core State Standards (CCSS). The chart on page 5 lists the anchor standards. The chart is also on the Digital Resource CD (filename: standards.pdf).

NAME: _____ **DATE:** _____

DIRECTIONS Read and answer each question.

1. Ⓨ Ⓝ

1. Write the missing punctuation in the sentence.

Americas first spy went to work during the Revolutionary War.

2. Ⓨ Ⓝ

2. Write the missing punctuation in the sentence.

He was a teacher until the war broke out and then he joined the militia.

3. Ⓨ Ⓝ

3. Circle the word that should be capitalized in the sentence.

Nathan Hale disguised himself as a dutch teacher.

4. Ⓨ Ⓝ

4. Underline the adjectives in sentence A below.

5. Ⓨ Ⓝ

5. Circle the verb in sentence A below.

6. Ⓨ Ⓝ

Ⓐ The British discovered his true identity.

7. Ⓨ Ⓝ

6. Underline the proper noun in sentence B below.

7. Circle the article in sentence B below.

8. Ⓨ Ⓝ

Ⓑ He was hanged by the British at age 21.

___ / 8
Total

8. Circle the word below that is spelled correctly.

inteligent   intellugent   intelligent

NAME: _____ DATE: _____

DIRECTIONS Read and answer each question.

1. Write the missing punctuation in the sentence.

"Ouch I just got scratched by a thorn," Marnie said.

1. Ⓨ Ⓝ

2. Write the missing punctuation in the sentence.

"Actually those aren't really thorns," Pedro pointed out.

2. Ⓨ Ⓝ

3. Ⓨ Ⓝ

3. Circle the word that should be capitalized in the sentence.

Marnie and Pedro were at the Municipal gardens.

4. Ⓨ Ⓝ

4. Underline the conjunction in sentence A below.

5. Ⓨ Ⓝ

5. Circle the proper noun in sentence A below.

Ⓐ "What are they called if they aren't thorns?" asked Marnie.

6. Ⓨ Ⓝ

6. Underline the linking verb in sentence B below.

7. Ⓨ Ⓝ

7. Circle the plural noun in sentence B below.

Ⓑ "They are prickles, but they still hurt!" said Pedro.

8. Ⓨ Ⓝ

8. Circle the word below that is spelled correctly.

cautiuos

cautious

cautous

___ / 8
Total

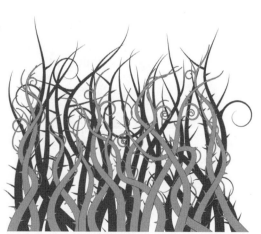

NAME: _____ DATE: _____

Read and answer each question.

SCORE

1. Ⓨ Ⓝ

2. Ⓨ Ⓝ

3. Ⓨ Ⓝ

4. Ⓨ Ⓝ

5. Ⓨ Ⓝ

6. Ⓨ Ⓝ

7. Ⓨ Ⓝ

8. Ⓨ Ⓝ

___ / 8
Total

1. Write the missing punctuation in the sentence.

Edgar Degas born in 1834, became a famous painter.

2. Write the missing punctuation in the sentence.

During his early years of painting he wanted to be a history painter.

3. Circle the word that should be capitalized in the sentence.

He practiced by painting in a museum called the louvre.

4. Underline the adverb in sentence A below.

5. Circle the plural noun in sentence A below.

A   Degas is very famous for paintings of dancers.

6. Underline the verb in sentence B below.

7. Circle the possessive pronoun in sentence B below.

B   You can see his works in many museums.

8. Circle the word below that is spelled correctly.

magnifucent

magnificient

magnificent

NAME: _____ DATE: _____

DIRECTIONS Read and answer each question.

1. Write the missing punctuation in the sentence.

J Patrick Lewis once saw a white rainbow.

1. Ⓨ Ⓝ

2. Write the missing punctuation in the sentence.

Also known as a fog bow it inspired Lewis.

2. Ⓨ Ⓝ

3. Ⓨ Ⓝ

3. Circle the words that should be capitalized in the sentence.

He wrote his first children's book, a russian folktale.

4. Ⓨ Ⓝ

4. Underline the possessive pronoun in sentence A below.

5. Ⓨ Ⓝ

5. Circle the plural nouns in sentence A below.

Ⓐ Publishers rejected his first story for seven years.

6. Ⓨ Ⓝ

6. Circle the title in sentence B below.

7. Ⓨ Ⓝ

7. Underline the verb in sentence B below.

Ⓑ He now has more than 80 books in print, such as Monumental Verses.

8. Ⓨ Ⓝ

8. Circle the word below that is spelled correctly.

___ / 8
Total

excellence   excellance   excelence

NAME: _____ **DATE:** _____

DIRECTIONS Read and answer each question.

1. Write the missing punctuation in the sentence.

1. Ⓨ Ⓝ

If he really existed Robin Hood lived in the year 1225.

2. Write the missing punctuation in the sentence.

2. Ⓨ Ⓝ

One man, a robbery suspect had a name similar to Robin Hood.

3. Ⓨ Ⓝ

3. Circle the word that should be capitalized in the sentence.

4. Ⓨ Ⓝ

This man lived near Sherwood forest, in England.

5. Ⓨ Ⓝ

4. Underline the pronoun in sentence A below.

5. Circle the conjunction in sentence A below.

6. Ⓨ Ⓝ

Ⓐ He was called a forester and an outlaw.

7. Ⓨ Ⓝ

6. Underline the contraction in sentence B below.

7. Circle the proper noun in sentence B below.

8. Ⓨ Ⓝ

Ⓑ Historians can't tell whether Robin Hood was a real person.

___ / 8
Total

8. Circle the word below that is spelled correctly.

deavious

devious

deveous

NAME: _____ **DATE:** _____

DIRECTIONS Read and answer each question.

1. Write the missing punctuation in the sentence.

More than 100 years ago, on a dark night a writer stared at Mars.

2. Write the missing punctuation in the sentence.

As he looked through a telescope, H. G Wells thought about Mars.

3. Circle the word that should be capitalized in the sentence.

His thoughts led him to write the book <u>the War of the Worlds</u>.

4. Underline the adjectives in sentence A below.

5. Circle the helping verb in sentence A below.

A Years later, this story of a Martian invasion was read on the radio.

6. Underline the article in sentence B below.

7. Circle the conjunction in sentence B below.

B Listeners thought the invasion was real, and thousands of people panicked.

8. Circle the word below that is spelled correctly.

anxiuos

anxious

anxoius

1. Ⓨ Ⓝ
2. Ⓨ Ⓝ
3. Ⓨ Ⓝ
4. Ⓨ Ⓝ
5. Ⓨ Ⓝ
6. Ⓨ Ⓝ
7. Ⓨ Ⓝ
8. Ⓨ Ⓝ

___ / 8
Total

NAME: _____ **DATE:** _____

DIRECTIONS Read and answer each question.

1. Ⓨ Ⓝ

1. Write the missing punctuation in the sentence.

Do you watch television shows about hospitals or crime

2. Ⓨ Ⓝ

2. Write the missing punctuation in the sentence.

A lot of what you see, such as blood and injuries is fake.

3. Ⓨ Ⓝ

3. Circle the word that should be capitalized in the sentence.

Michael crichton, a writer and a TV producer, went to medical school.

4. Ⓨ Ⓝ

4. Underline the possessive pronoun in sentence A below.

5. Circle the plural noun in sentence A below.

5. Ⓨ Ⓝ

6. Ⓨ Ⓝ

A Medical school prepared him for writing his realistic stories.

7. Ⓨ Ⓝ

6. Underline the verbs in sentence B below.

7. Circle the pronoun in sentence B below.

8. Ⓨ Ⓝ

B He wrote novels to pay his way through school.

___ / 8
Total

8. Circle the word below that is spelled correctly.

guidance   guidence   giudance

NAME: _____ DATE: _____

DIRECTIONS Read and answer each question.

1. Write the missing punctuation in the sentence.

Years ago, people used cowrie shells cacao beans, and wheat for money.

1. Ⓨ Ⓝ

2. Write the missing punctuation in the sentence.

2. Ⓨ Ⓝ

Wampum, which was exchanged by American Indians was made of polished beads from shells.

3. Ⓨ Ⓝ

3. Circle the word that should be capitalized in the sentence.

4. Ⓨ Ⓝ

The aztecs in Central Mexico used cacao beans when shopping.

5. Ⓨ Ⓝ

4. Underline the complete subject in sentence A below.

5. Circle the helping verb in sentence A below.

6. Ⓨ Ⓝ

Ⓐ Cacao beans were used for making chocolate.

7. Ⓨ Ⓝ

6. Underline the conjunction in sentence B below.

7. Circle the possessive pronoun in sentence B below.

8. Ⓨ Ⓝ

Ⓑ It would be great if you could grow your own money!

___ / 8
Total

8. Circle the word below that is spelled correctly.

prefered   preferred   prefrered

NAME: _____ DATE: _____

DIRECTIONS Read and answer each question.

SCORE

1. Y N

1. Write the missing punctuation in the sentence.

If you think climbing walls is a new idea, youd be wrong.

2. Y N

2. Write the missing punctuation in the sentence.

In 1939, Clark Schurman made the first wall climb in Seattle Washington.

3. Y N

3. Circle the words that should be capitalized in the sentence.

Clark Schurman was a boy scout leader who loved climbing.

4. Y N

4. Underline the article in sentence A below.

5. Y N

5. Circle the pronoun in sentence A below.

6. Y N

A He called the climbing structure Monitor Rock.

7. Y N

6. Underline the prepositional phrase in sentence B below.

7. Circle the helping verb in sentence B below.

8. Y N

B After his death, the rock was renamed Schurman Rock.

___ / 8
Total

8. Circle the word below that is spelled correctly.

equiptment   equipmeant   equipment

NAME: _____ **DATE:** _____

DIRECTIONS Read and answer each question.

1. Write the missing punctuation in the sentence.

In 1955 Maurice Sendak was working on a children's book.

1. Ⓨ Ⓝ

2. Write the missing punctuation in the sentence.

At first he called the book <u>Where the Wild Horses Are</u>.

2. Ⓨ Ⓝ

3. Ⓨ Ⓝ

3. Circle the word that should be capitalized in the sentence.

Then he tried <u>Where the Wild Animals are</u>.

4. Ⓨ Ⓝ

4. Underline the pronoun in sentence A below.

5. Ⓨ Ⓝ

5. Circle the adverb in sentence A below.

Ⓐ Finally, he changed the title to <u>Where the Wild Things Are</u>.

6. Ⓨ Ⓝ

6. Underline the linking verb in sentence B below.

7. Ⓨ Ⓝ

7. Circle the preposition in sentence B below.

Ⓑ Sendak was 83 when he died on May 8, 2012.

8. Ⓨ Ⓝ

8. Circle the word below that is spelled correctly.

mischief   mischeif   mischiuf

___ / 8
Total

NAME: _____   **DATE:** _____

1. Ⓨ Ⓝ

2. Ⓨ Ⓝ

3. Ⓨ Ⓝ

4. Ⓨ Ⓝ

5. Ⓨ Ⓝ

6. Ⓨ Ⓝ

7. Ⓨ Ⓝ

8. Ⓨ Ⓝ

___ / 8
Total

DIRECTIONS Read and answer each question.

1. Write the missing punctuation in the sentence.

The Tower of London, with its huge walls is more than a tower.

2. Write the missing punctuation in the sentence.

In the 1070s William the Conqueror started building the fortress.

3. Circle the word that should be capitalized in the sentence.

It was built on the thames, a river, and looks a lot like a castle.

4. Underline the verb in sentence A below.

5. Circle the compound subject in sentence A below.

Ⓐ Kings and queens often took refuge there.

6. Underline the adverb in sentence B below.

7. Circle the pronoun in sentence B below.

Ⓑ Sometimes, they were imprisoned or executed there.

8. Circle the word below that is spelled correctly.

centureis

centuries

centeuries

NAME: _____ **DATE:** _____

DIRECTIONS Read and answer each question.

SCORE

1. Write the missing punctuation in the sentence.

Sometimes we worry about big things and sometimes we worry about small things.

2. Write the missing punctuation in the sentence.

Doctors, as it happens worry about some of the trillions of microbes in your body.

3. Circle the word that should be capitalized in the sentence.

One virus, named after the ebola River, caused hundreds of deaths in 1976.

4. Underline the adverb in sentence A below.

5. Circle the plural noun in sentence A below.

A Scientists study the virus closely because it is deadly.

6. Underline the verb in sentence B below.

7. Circle the prepositional phrase in sentence B below.

B In 2014, an outbreak of the disease made people very nervous.

8. Circle the word below that is spelled correctly.

occurence

occurrence

ocurrence

SCORE

1. Ⓨ Ⓝ

2. Ⓨ Ⓝ

3. Ⓨ Ⓝ

4. Ⓨ Ⓝ

5. Ⓨ Ⓝ

6. Ⓨ Ⓝ

7. Ⓨ Ⓝ

8. Ⓨ Ⓝ

___ / 8
Total

NAME: _____ **DATE:** _____

DIRECTIONS Read and answer each question.

1. Ⓨ Ⓝ

2. Ⓨ Ⓝ

3. Ⓨ Ⓝ

4. Ⓨ Ⓝ

5. Ⓨ Ⓝ

6. Ⓨ Ⓝ

7. Ⓨ Ⓝ

8. Ⓨ Ⓝ

___ / 8
Total

1. Write the missing punctuation in the sentence.

Do you do "the wave at football games?

2. Write the missing punctuation in the sentence.

The wave was first seen on television on October 15 1981.

3. Circle the word that should be capitalized in the sentence.

George Henderson, a big fan, first started it at San Jose State university.

4. Underline the verbs in sentence A below.

5. Circle the proper noun in sentence A below.

A Henderson had fans stand up and cheer, one section at a time.

6. Underline the article in sentence B below.

7. Circle the pronoun in sentence B below.

B It caught on after being seen during a baseball playoff game.

8. Circle the word below that is spelled correctly.

joyous   joyuos   joyuss

NAME: _____ **DATE:** _____

DIRECTIONS Read and answer each question.

SCORE

1. Write the missing punctuation in the sentence.

What did you toss in todays garbage?

2. Write the missing punctuation in the sentence.

Did you throw away paper food, or a plastic bottle?

3. Circle the word that should be capitalized in the sentence.

Dr. william I. Rathje digs through garbage that is decades old.

4. Underline the possessive pronoun in sentence A below.

5. Circle the conjunction in sentence A below.

A His students help him dig up landfills and study the garbage.

6. Underline the adverb in sentence B below.

7. Circle the proper noun in sentence B below.

B They could easily read Christmas cards buried for 30 years.

8. Circle the word below that is spelled correctly.

regrettible

regretable

regrettable

1. Ⓨ Ⓝ

2. Ⓨ Ⓝ

3. Ⓨ Ⓝ

4. Ⓨ Ⓝ

5. Ⓨ Ⓝ

6. Ⓨ Ⓝ

7. Ⓨ Ⓝ

8. Ⓨ Ⓝ

___ / 8
Total

NAME: _____ **DATE:** _____

1. Ⓨ Ⓝ

2. Ⓨ Ⓝ

3. Ⓨ Ⓝ

4. Ⓨ Ⓝ

5. Ⓨ Ⓝ

6. Ⓨ Ⓝ

7. Ⓨ Ⓝ

8. Ⓨ Ⓝ

___ / 8
Total

DIRECTIONS Read and answer each question.

1. Write the missing punctuation in the sentence.

Have you heard the story about the vanishing hitchhiker

2. Write the missing punctuation in the sentence.

Stories like these can be scary funny, or hard to believe.

3. Circle the word that should be capitalized in the sentence.

Jan harold Brunvand studies stories like these.

4. Underline the plural noun in sentence A below.

5. Circle the plural pronoun in sentence A below.

A They are called modern urban legends.

6. Underline the verb in sentence B below.

7. Circle the adverb in sentence B below.

B The stories usually come from a friend of a friend.

8. Circle the word below that is spelled correctly.

incredeble

incredable

incredible

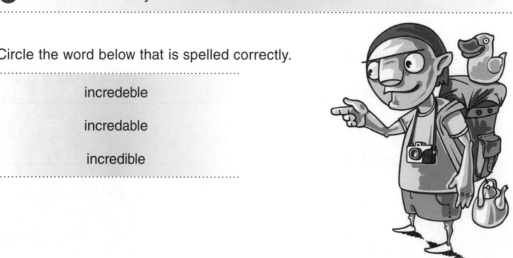

#51170—180 Days of Language

NAME: _____ DATE: _____

Read and answer each question.

SCORE

1. Write the missing punctuation in the sentence.

Do you like to tell jokes, riddles, or puns

1. Ⓨ Ⓝ

2. Write the missing punctuation in the sentence.

Jamie said, "What do you call an overweight feline?

2. Ⓨ Ⓝ

3. Ⓨ Ⓝ

3. Circle the word that should be capitalized in the sentence.

Cerillo said, "a fat cat!"

4. Ⓨ Ⓝ

4. Underline the helping verb in sentence A below.

5. Ⓨ Ⓝ

5. Circle the adjective in sentence A below.

Ⓐ These riddles are called hink-pinks.

6. Ⓨ Ⓝ

6. Underline the conjunction in sentence B below.

7. Ⓨ Ⓝ

7. Circle the prepositional phrase in sentence B below.

Ⓑ The answer rhymes and has one syllable in each word.

8. Ⓨ Ⓝ

8. Circle the word below that is spelled correctly.

___ / 8
Total

entertainment

entertanement

entertaiment

NAME: _____ DATE: _____

DIRECTIONS Read and answer each question.

1. (Y)(N)

1. Write the missing punctuation in the sentence.

Crazy Horse, an American Indian warrior was a brave man.

2. (Y)(N)

2. Write the missing punctuation in the sentence.

He didnt want American Indians to give up their ways of life.

3. (Y)(N)

3. Circle the word that should be capitalized in the sentence.

4. (Y)(N)

He fought bravely with Sitting bull at Little Bighorn.

5. (Y)(N)

4. Underline the prepositional phrase in sentence A below.

5. Circle the pronoun in sentence A below.

6. (Y)(N)

A His father had the same name of Crazy Horse.

7. (Y)(N)

6. Underline the adverb in sentence B below.

7. Circle the conjunction in sentence B below.

8. (Y)(N)

B He surrendered to troops in 1877 but was soon killed.

___ / 8
Total

8. Circle the word below that is spelled correctly.

difiance   defieance   defiance

NAME: _____ **DATE:** _____

DIRECTIONS Read and answer each question.

1. Write the missing punctuation in the sentence.

Pietra said, I just learned something about the author of <u>Peter Pan</u>."

2. Write the missing punctuation in the sentence.

Mrs Lucero asked, "What did you learn, Pietra?"

3. Circle the word that should be capitalized in the sentence.

"J. M. Barrie sometimes got writer's cramp," pietra said.

4. Underline the conjunction in sentence A below.

5. Circle the pronoun in sentence A below.

A "He would switch hands and keep writing!" Pietra exclaimed.

6. Underline the proper noun in sentence B below.

7. Circle the adverb in sentence B below.

B "He also said his writing style changed with his left hand," Pietra added.

8. Circle the word below that is spelled correctly.

flexibel   flexible   flexable

1. Y N

2. Y N

3. Y N

4. Y N

5. Y N

6. Y N

7. Y N

8. Y N

___ / 8
Total

NAME: _____ **DATE:** _____

SCORE

DIRECTIONS Read and answer each question.

1. Ⓨ Ⓝ

1. Write the missing punctuation in the sentence.

If you haven't read a book by Mark Twain you may not know about the author's name.

2. Ⓨ Ⓝ

2. Write the missing punctuation in the sentence.

Born on November 30, 1835 Samuel Langhorne Clemens had several jobs.

3. Ⓨ Ⓝ

3. Circle the word that should be capitalized in the sentence.

He became a riverboat pilot on the Mississippi river.

4. Ⓨ Ⓝ

4. Underline the article in sentence A below.

5. Ⓨ Ⓝ

5. Circle the verbs in sentence A below.

Ⓐ *Mark twain* means the water was two fathoms deep.

6. Ⓨ Ⓝ

6. Underline the adjectives in sentence B below.

7. Ⓨ Ⓝ

7. Circle the verb in sentence B below.

Ⓑ He adopted the words for his pen name.

8. Ⓨ Ⓝ

_____ / 8
Total

8. Circle the word below that is spelled correctly.

preferanse

preference

preference

 #51170—180 Days of Language

NAME: _____ **DATE:** _____

DIRECTIONS Read and answer each question.

1. Write the missing punctuation in the sentence.

In 1865 the Central Pacific Railroad track was under construction.

1. Ⓨ Ⓝ

2. Write the missing punctuation in the sentence.

The builders needed cheap labor so they hired many immigrants.

2. Ⓨ Ⓝ

3. Ⓨ Ⓝ

3. Circle the words that should be capitalized in the sentence.

By 1868, thousands of chinese and irish workers had been hired.

4. Ⓨ Ⓝ

4. Underline the prepositional phrase in sentence A below.

5. Ⓨ Ⓝ

5. Circle the adjectives in sentence A below.

Ⓐ   The workers set a new record for laying track.

6. Ⓨ Ⓝ

6. Underline the complete subject in sentence B below.

7. Ⓨ Ⓝ

7. Circle the verb in sentence B below.

Ⓑ   They laid more than ten miles of track in about twelve hours!

8. Ⓨ Ⓝ

8. Circle the word below that is spelled correctly.

_____ / 8
Total

unbroken   unbrokin   unnbroken

DIRECTIONS Read and answer each question.

SCORE

1. Ⓨ Ⓝ

1. Write the missing punctuation in the sentence.

Christopher Paul Curtis didnt start out as a writer.

2. Ⓨ Ⓝ

2. Write the missing punctuation in the sentence.

For thirteen years he hung doors on cars on an assembly line.

3. Ⓨ Ⓝ

3. Circle the word that should be capitalized in the sentence.

"I can't tell you how much I hated it," curtis said.

4. Ⓨ Ⓝ

4. Circle the title in sentence A below.

5. Ⓨ Ⓝ

5. Underline the prepositional phrase in sentence A below.

6. Ⓨ Ⓝ

A In his spare time, he wrote The Watsons Go to Birmingham—1963.

7. Ⓨ Ⓝ

6. Underline the verb in sentence B below.

7. Circle the possessive pronoun in sentence B below.

8. Ⓨ Ⓝ

B His second book, Bud, Not Buddy, won the Newbery Medal.

___ / 8
Total

8. Circle the word below that is spelled correctly.

dilligent   diligent   dilegent

NAME: _____ DATE: _____

DIRECTIONS Read and answer each question.

1. Write the missing punctuation in the sentence.

During the War of 1812 the British burned the capitol in Washington, D.C.

1. Ⓨ Ⓝ

2. Write the missing comma in the sentence.

A library with 3000 books was also destroyed.

2. Ⓨ Ⓝ

3. Ⓨ Ⓝ

3. Circle the word that should be capitalized in the sentence.

Thomas Jefferson, a former United states president, was upset by this.

4. Ⓨ Ⓝ

4. Underline the conjunction in sentence A below.

5. Ⓨ Ⓝ

5. Circle the pronoun in sentence A below.

A Jefferson owned 6,707 books, and he had bills to pay.

6. Ⓨ Ⓝ

6. Underline the verb in sentence B below.

7. Ⓨ Ⓝ

7. Circle the possessive noun in sentence B below.

B The United States Congress bought Jefferson's library for $23,950.

8. Ⓨ Ⓝ

8. Circle the word below that is spelled correctly.

remarkable   remarkible   remarkkable

___ / 8
Total

NAME: _____ DATE: _____

DIRECTIONS Read and answer each question.

1. (Y)(N)

1. Write the missing punctuation in the sentence.

If you like nonsense rhymes you will like Edward Lear.

2. (Y)(N)

2. Write the missing punctuation in the sentence.

Born in 1812 he was one of 21 children!

3. (Y)(N)

3. Circle the word that should be capitalized in the sentence.

4. (Y)(N)

Edward lived in london and was often sick as a child.

5. (Y)(N)

4. Underline the conjunction in sentence A below.

5. Circle the verbs in sentence A below.

6. (Y)(N)

A He loved painting, but he never became famous as an artist.

7. (Y)(N)

6. Underline the prepositional phrase in sentence B below.

7. Circle the adjectives in sentence B below.

8. (Y)(N)

B He did become famous for his funny limericks.

___ / 8
Total

8. Circle the word below that is spelled correctly.

amusment

amusemant

amusement

NAME: _____ **DATE:** _____

DIRECTIONS Read and answer each question.

1. Write the missing punctuation in the sentence.

In 1856, Frank Baum was born in Chittenango New York.

2. Write the missing punctuation in the sentence.

For years he managed theaters and worked as an actor.

3. Circle the word that should be capitalized in the sentence.

He had a hard time getting <u>the Wonderful Wizard of Oz</u> published.

4. Underline the contraction in sentence A below.

5. Circle the adverb in sentence A below.

A Publishers mistakenly thought children wouldn't like the book.

6. Underline the adverb in sentence B below.

7. Circle the verb in sentence B below.

B Baum finally paid all of the publishing costs.

8. Circle the word below that is spelled correctly.

boastfull

boastful

bosteful

1. Ⓨ Ⓝ

2. Ⓨ Ⓝ

3. Ⓨ Ⓝ

4. Ⓨ Ⓝ

5. Ⓨ Ⓝ

6. Ⓨ Ⓝ

7. Ⓨ Ⓝ

8. Ⓨ Ⓝ

___ / 8
Total

NAME: _____ DATE: _____

DIRECTIONS Read and answer each question.

1. (Y)(N)

1. Write the missing punctuation in the sentence.

Do you have pennies, nickels dimes, or quarters in your pocket?

2. (Y)(N)

2. Write the missing punctuation in the sentence.

In 1866 the first nickel was issued.

3. (Y)(N)

3. Circle the word that should be capitalized in the sentence.

It was issued by the U.S. mint.

4. (Y)(N)

4. Underline the contraction in sentence A below.

5. Circle the conjunction in sentence A below.

5. (Y)(N)

6. (Y)(N)

A Nickel is a metal, but the coin wasn't all nickel.

7. (Y)(N)

6. Underline the linking verb in sentence B below.

7. Circle the article in sentence B below.

8. (Y)(N)

B The first nickel was 25 percent nickel and 75 percent copper, making it stronger.

___ / 8
Total

8. Circle the word below that is spelled correctly.

strengthen

strengthin

strongthen

NAME: _____ **DATE:** _____

DIRECTIONS Read and answer each question.

1. Write the missing punctuation in the sentence.

If you want to see the largest Tyrannosaurus rex go to Chicago.

2. Write the missing punctuation in the sentence.

Called Sue she is 42 feet long and 13 feet high.

3. Circle the word that should be capitalized in the sentence.

You can usually see Sue at the Field museum.

4. Underline the adverb in sentence A below.

5. Circle the proper noun in sentence A below.

A Sometimes, Sue is part of a traveling exhibit.

6. Underline the preposition in sentence B below.

7. Circle the common nouns in sentence B below.

B Maybe Sue will visit a museum in your city!

8. Circle the word below that is spelled correctly.

discouvery   descovery   discovery

1. Ⓨ Ⓝ

2. Ⓨ Ⓝ

3. Ⓨ Ⓝ

4. Ⓨ Ⓝ

5. Ⓨ Ⓝ

6. Ⓨ Ⓝ

7. Ⓨ Ⓝ

8. Ⓨ Ⓝ

___ / 8
Total

NAME: _____ **DATE:** _____

1. Ⓨ Ⓝ

2. Ⓨ Ⓝ

3. Ⓨ Ⓝ

4. Ⓨ Ⓝ

5. Ⓨ Ⓝ

6. Ⓨ Ⓝ

7. Ⓨ Ⓝ

8. Ⓨ Ⓝ

___ / 8
Total

DIRECTIONS   Read and answer each question.

1. Write the missing punctuation in the sentence.

If Ben Franklin had gotten his way the turkey would be the national bird.

2. Write the missing punctuation in the sentence.

Franklin thought that the bald eagle, our national bird had bad character.

3. Circle the word that should be capitalized in the sentence.

About 46 to 50 million turkeys are sold each year for thanksgiving.

4. Underline the contraction in sentence A below.

5. Circle the conjunction in sentence A below.

Ⓐ   Tom turkeys gobble, but hens don't.

6. Underline the adjectives in sentence B below.

7. Circle the possessive noun in sentence B below.

Ⓑ   The red wattle on a turkey's neck can represent its mood.

8. Circle the word below that is spelled correctly.

vegitable

vegetable

vegetible

NAME: _____ **DATE:** _____

DIRECTIONS   Read and answer each question.

1. Write the missing punctuation in the sentence.

When you get on a plane you might not worry about other flying things.

2. Write the missing punctuation in the sentence.

However birds can be a big problem for pilots.

3. Circle the word that should be capitalized in the sentence.

Birds such as canada geese have damaged plane engines.

4. Underline the verb in sentence A below.

5. Circle the adverb in sentence A below.

A   Many airports work hard to keep the birds away.

6. Underline the plural noun in sentence B below.

7. Circle the conjunction in sentence B below.

B   Radar helps, too, because it shows where the birds are.

8. Circle the word below that is spelled correctly.

accidant   accident   acident

1. Ⓨ Ⓝ

2. Ⓨ Ⓝ

3. Ⓨ Ⓝ

4. Ⓨ Ⓝ

5. Ⓨ Ⓝ

6. Ⓨ Ⓝ

7. Ⓨ Ⓝ

8. Ⓨ Ⓝ

___ / 8
Total

NAME: _____ DATE: _____

DIRECTIONS Read and answer each question.

1. Ⓨ Ⓝ

2. Ⓨ Ⓝ

3. Ⓨ Ⓝ

4. Ⓨ Ⓝ

5. Ⓨ Ⓝ

6. Ⓨ Ⓝ

7. Ⓨ Ⓝ

8. Ⓨ Ⓝ

___ / 8
Total

1. Write the missing punctuation in the sentence.

For thousands of years people have been lifting weights.

2. Write the missing punctuation in the sentence.

Weightlifters can be seen in ancient paintings sculptures, and drawings.

3. Circle the word that should be capitalized in the sentence.

Soldiers in ancient china had to pass lifting tests.

4. Underline the complete subject in sentence A below.

5. Circle the conjunction in sentence A below.

A People lifted stones at first and later lifted dumbbells.

6. Underline the prepositional phrase in sentence B below.

7. Circle the article in sentence B below.

B The clappers were removed from bells, making them soundless.

8. Circle the word below that is spelled correctly.

glorrious

glorius

glorious

NAME: _____ **DATE:** _____

DIRECTIONS Read and answer each question.

SCORE

1. Write the missing punctuation in the sentence.

Charles Lindbergh, a pilot was famous for his flying.

2. Write the missing punctuation in the sentence.

However his life changed completely one day in 1932.

3. Circle the word that should be capitalized in the sentence.

His son, charles Junior, was kidnapped.

4. Underline the verb in sentence A below.

5. Circle the proper noun in sentence A below.

A The trial of Richard Bruno Hauptmann fascinated the nation.

6. Underline the article in sentence B below.

7. Circle the introductory clause in sentence B below.

B Although found guilty, people still wondered if Hauptmann kidnapped the baby.

8. Circle the word below that is spelled correctly.

accuse

acuse

accusse

SCORE

1. Ⓨ Ⓝ

2. Ⓨ Ⓝ

3. Ⓨ Ⓝ

4. Ⓨ Ⓝ

5. Ⓨ Ⓝ

6. Ⓨ Ⓝ

7. Ⓨ Ⓝ

8. Ⓨ Ⓝ

___ / 8
Total

NAME: _____   DATE: _____

DIRECTIONS   Read and answer each question.

SCORE

1. Ⓨ Ⓝ

1. Write the missing punctuation in the sentence.

On April 22 1970, the first Earth Day was held.

2. Ⓨ Ⓝ

2. Write the missing punctuation in the sentence.

Gaylord Nelson, a U.S. senator was worried about pollution.

3. Ⓨ Ⓝ

3. Circle the word that should be capitalized in the sentence.

There had been a massive oil spill in santa Barbara, California.

4. Ⓨ Ⓝ

4. Underline the proper noun in sentence A below.

5. Ⓨ Ⓝ

5. Circle the prepositional phrases in sentence A below.

6. Ⓨ Ⓝ

Ⓐ   Senator Nelson wanted people to think about pollution.

7. Ⓨ Ⓝ

6. Underline the prepositional phrase in sentence B below.

7. Circle the possessive noun in sentence B below.

8. Ⓨ Ⓝ

Ⓑ   One man's idea has spread around the world.

___ / 8
Total

8. Circle the word below that is spelled correctly.

environement

environment

envirunment

#51170—180 Days of Language

NAME: _____ **DATE:** _____

DIRECTIONS Read and answer each question.

1. Write the missing punctuation in the sentence.

Theres nothing more fun than a puppy, right?

1. Ⓨ Ⓝ

2. Write the missing punctuation in the sentence.

However maybe owning a puppy isn't right for you.

2. Ⓨ Ⓝ

3. Ⓨ Ⓝ

3. Circle the word that should be capitalized in the sentence.

In many cities, such as chicago, you can help by being a foster caregiver.

4. Ⓨ Ⓝ

4. Underline the conjunction in sentence A below.

5. Ⓨ Ⓝ

5. Circle the verb in sentence A below.

6. Ⓨ Ⓝ

A You can foster a dog or a cat for a while.

6. Underline the adjectives in sentence B below.

7. Ⓨ Ⓝ

7. Circle the contraction in sentence B below.

8. Ⓨ Ⓝ

B You'll make a great friend and have fun, too!

____ / 8
Total

8. Circle the word below that is spelled correctly.

adaupt   adoup   adopt

NAME: _____ DATE: _____

DIRECTIONS Read and answer each question.

1. Write the missing punctuation in the sentence.

For many years inventors worked on making washing machines.

1. (Y) (N)

2. Write the missing punctuation in the sentence.

However, it wasnt until 1874 that a good machine was made.

2. (Y) (N)

3. (Y) (N)

3. Circle the word that should be capitalized in the sentence.

That year, william Blackstone gave a birthday present to his wife.

4. (Y) (N)

4. Underline the conjunction in sentence A below.

5. (Y) (N)

5. Circle the adverb in sentence A below.

A That machine worked well, and other people wanted one.

6. (Y) (N)

6. Underline the preposition in sentence B below.

7. (Y) (N)

7. Circle the pronoun in sentence B below.

8. (Y) (N)

B After five years, he opened a washing machine factory.

___ / 8
Total

8. Circle the word below that is spelled correctly.

clothesline

closeline

clothsline

#51170—180 Days of Language

NAME: _____ DATE: _____

DIRECTIONS Read and answer each question.

1. Write the missing punctuation in the sentence.

Do you like hip-hop ballet, or ballroom dancing?

2. Write the missing punctuation in the sentence.

Breakdancing was popular in cities such as New York City New York.

3. Circle the word that should be capitalized in the sentence.

Funk-style dancing developed in california at about the same time.

4. Underline the plural noun in sentence A below.

5. Circle the singular noun in sentence A below.

A A dancer may combine different styles.

6. Underline the adjectives in sentence B below.

7. Circle the conjunction in sentence B below.

B Dancing can be creative, and it can be fun.

8. Circle the word below that is spelled correctly.

gracfully   gracefully   gracefuly

1. Ⓨ Ⓝ

2. Ⓨ Ⓝ

3. Ⓨ Ⓝ

4. Ⓨ Ⓝ

5. Ⓨ Ⓝ

6. Ⓨ Ⓝ

7. Ⓨ Ⓝ

8. Ⓨ Ⓝ

___ / 8
Total

NAME: _____ **DATE:** _____

DIRECTIONS Read and answer each question.

1. Ⓨ Ⓝ

2. Ⓨ Ⓝ

3. Ⓨ Ⓝ

4. Ⓨ Ⓝ

5. Ⓨ Ⓝ

6. Ⓨ Ⓝ

7. Ⓨ Ⓝ

8. Ⓨ Ⓝ

___ / 8
Total

1. Write the missing punctuation in the sentence.

For three weeks each summer about 200 racers bike through France.

2. Write the missing punctuation in the sentence.

Racers bike on flat hilly, and mountain roads.

3. Circle the word that should be capitalized in the sentence.

The race, called the tour de France, began in 1903.

4. Underline the verb in sentence A below.

5. Circle the complete subject in sentence A below.

Ⓐ   The route changes from year to year.

6. Underline the prepositional phrase in sentence B below.

7. Circle the article in sentence B below.

Ⓑ   The racers who finish will have ridden about 2,000 miles.

8. Circle the word below that is spelled correctly.

kicksand

kikstand

kickstand

NAME: _____ **DATE:** _____

DIRECTIONS Read and answer each question.

1. Write the missing punctuation in the sentence.

People who work digs are called archaeologists and they never know what they will find.

2. Write the missing punctuation in the sentence.

They might find rare art gold, or even a mummy!

3. Circle the word that should be capitalized in the sentence.

During a dig in Knossos, crete, an entire palace was found!

4. Underline the complete subject in sentence A below.

5. Circle the adjectives in sentence A below.

A The huge palace was built about 3,500 years ago.

6. Underline the adverb in sentence B below.

7. Circle the verb in sentence B below.

B More than 4,000 people probably lived in the palace.

8. Circle the word below that is spelled correctly.

skeleton

skeliton

skeleten

NAME: _____ DATE: _____

DIRECTIONS Read and answer each question.

1. Ⓨ Ⓝ

2. Ⓨ Ⓝ

3. Ⓨ Ⓝ

4. Ⓨ Ⓝ

5. Ⓨ Ⓝ

6. Ⓨ Ⓝ

7. Ⓨ Ⓝ

8. Ⓨ Ⓝ

___ / 8
Total

1. Write the missing punctuation in the sentence.

You can touch your fingers with your thumbs which are sometimes called opposable thumbs.

2. Write the missing punctuation in the sentence.

Some animals, such as great apes have opposable thumbs on both their hands and feet.

3. Circle the word that should be capitalized in the sentence.

Others with opposable thumbs include Old world monkeys.

4. Underline the verb in sentence A below.

5. Circle the adverb in sentence A below.

A Chimps sometimes use stones as hammers.

6. Underline the prepositional phrase in sentence B below.

7. Circle the complete subject in sentence B below.

B Some monkeys crack nuts with stones.

8. Circle the word below that is spelled correctly.

thumbnaile   thumbnail   thumbnale

NAME: _____ DATE: _____

DIRECTIONS Read and answer each question.

1. Write the missing punctuation in the sentence.

Do you use an e-reader a phone, or a computer for reading books?

1. Ⓨ Ⓝ

2. Write the missing punctuation in the sentence.

By sixth grade your backpack might weigh 20 pounds!

2. Ⓨ Ⓝ

3. Ⓨ Ⓝ

3. Circle the word that should be capitalized in the sentence.

Researchers in New York city schools weighed lots of students' backpacks.

4. Ⓨ Ⓝ

4. Underline the helping verb in sentence A below.

5. Ⓨ Ⓝ

5. Circle the adjective in sentence A below.

Ⓐ Heavy backpacks may cause pain.

6. Ⓨ Ⓝ

6. Underline the verb in sentence B below.

7. Ⓨ Ⓝ

7. Circle the preposition in sentence B below.

Ⓑ Some schools use e-books for a lighter load.

8. Ⓨ Ⓝ

8. Circle the word below that is spelled correctly.

textbouk

texbook

textbook

___ / 8
Total

NAME: _____ DATE: _____

DIRECTIONS Read and answer each question.

1. (Y)(N)

1. Write the missing punctuation in the sentence.

For four years the president of the United States has a big job.

2. (Y)(N)

2. Write the missing punctuation in the sentence.

The president, also serving as the commander in chief leads the government.

3. (Y)(N)

3. Circle the word that should be capitalized in the sentence.

He works with the senate and the House of Representatives.

4. (Y)(N)

4. Underline the prepositional phrase in sentence A below.

5. Circle the adjectives in sentence A below.

5. (Y)(N)

6. (Y)(N)

A All new laws must be signed by the president.

7. (Y)(N)

6. Underline the helping verb in sentence B below.

7. Circle the compound subject in sentence B below.

8. (Y)(N)

B He or she may run for a second term.

___ / 8
Total

8. Circle the word below that is spelled correctly.

vetoes   vetos   veetoes

NAME: _____ **DATE:** _____

DIRECTIONS Read and answer each question.

1. Write the missing punctuation in the sentence.

Have you ever thought about farming in the city

1. Ⓨ Ⓝ

2. Write the missing punctuation in the sentence.

Some teens spend their summers doing just that in Madison Wisconsin.

2. Ⓨ Ⓝ

3. Ⓨ Ⓝ

3. Circle the word that should be capitalized in the sentence.

They grow everything they need for salsa at the Darbo Community garden.

4. Ⓨ Ⓝ

4. Underline the verb in sentence A below.

5. Circle the nouns in sentence A below.

5. Ⓨ Ⓝ

A The teens grow most of the vegetables for the salsa.

6. Ⓨ Ⓝ

6. Underline the subject pronoun in sentence B below.

7. Ⓨ Ⓝ

7. Circle the possessive pronoun in sentence B below.

B They call their product Off the Block Salsa.

8. Ⓨ Ⓝ

8. Circle the word below that is spelled correctly.

____ / 8
Total

vacant

vaccant

vacante

NAME: _____ **DATE:** _____

DIRECTIONS Read and answer each question.

1. (Y) (N)

1. Write the missing punctuation in the sentence.

Thanks to the high cost of gas more people are buying electric cars.

2. (Y) (N)

2. Write the missing punctuation in the sentence.

These cars have a battery which must be charged.

3. (Y) (N)

3. Circle the word that should be capitalized in the sentence.

4. (Y) (N)

Many american drivers will buy one if it doesn't cost more.

5. (Y) (N)

4. Underline the helping verb in sentence A below.

5. Circle the complete subject in sentence A below.

6. (Y) (N)

A Drivers must pay for the electricity.

7. (Y) (N)

6. Underline the linking verb in sentence B below.

7. Circle the plural noun in sentence B below.

8. (Y) (N)

B Even with the cost of electricity, these cars are cheaper.

___ / 8
Total

8. Circle the word below that is spelled correctly.

reliable   relieble   reliuble

NAME: _____ DATE: _____

DIRECTIONS Read and answer each question.

1. Write the missing punctuation in the sentence.

Many people fear snakes such as the copperhead snake.

1. Ⓨ Ⓝ

2. Write the missing punctuation in the sentence.

With its orange coloring and brown markings, its easy to spot.

2. Ⓨ Ⓝ

3. Ⓨ Ⓝ

3. Circle the word that should be capitalized in the sentence.

Copperhead bites are not usually fatal, according to dr. Peter Bromley.

4. Ⓨ Ⓝ

4. Underline the adjectives in sentence A below.

5. Ⓨ Ⓝ

5. Circle the helping verb in sentence A below.

Ⓐ However, its bite can kill a small animal.

6. Ⓨ Ⓝ

6. Underline the contraction in sentence B below.

7. Ⓨ Ⓝ

7. Circle the conjunction in sentence B below.

Ⓑ Don't pick it up if you see one!

8. Ⓨ Ⓝ

8. Circle the word below that is spelled correctly.

___ / 8
Total

rattlesnake

rattelsnake

ratlesnake

NAME: _____ **DATE:** _____

1. Ⓨ Ⓝ

2. Ⓨ Ⓝ

3. Ⓨ Ⓝ

4. Ⓨ Ⓝ

5. Ⓨ Ⓝ

6. Ⓨ Ⓝ

7. Ⓨ Ⓝ

8. Ⓨ Ⓝ

___ / 8
Total

DIRECTIONS Read and answer each question.

1. Write the missing punctuation in the sentence.

Most of us recycle paper but do you think about tissue when you sneeze?

2. Write the missing punctuation in the sentence.

Of course, you dont want to pass along a cold with that tissue.

3. Circle the word that should be capitalized in the sentence.

People in the United states use more tissues than they do in other countries.

4. Underline the preposition in sentence A below.

5. Circle the plural nouns in sentence A below.

Ⓐ Those tissues come from trees that have been cut down.

6. Underline the adjective in sentence B below.

7. Circle the pronoun in sentence B below.

Ⓑ You can help by buying recycled tissues.

8. Circle the word below that is spelled correctly.

handkerchefe   handkercheif   handkerchief

NAME: _____ **DATE:** _____

DIRECTIONS   Read and answer each question.

1. Write the missing punctuation in the sentence.

When you have a birthday do you get a swat or a pinch for each year?

2. Write the missing punctuation in the sentence.

Birthday customs, such as giving bumps and thumps vary around the world.

3. Circle the word that should be capitalized in the sentence.

Kids in brazil get an earlobe pulled for each year.

4. Underline the proper noun in sentence A below.

5. Circle the plural noun in sentence A below.

A   Kids in Puerto Rico get tapped on the arm for each year.

6. Underline the helping verb in sentence B below.

7. Circle the conjunction in sentence B below.

B   These taps, bumps, and thumps are thought to be lucky.

8. Circle the word below that is spelled correctly.

occassion   occasion   ocassion

1. Ⓨ Ⓝ

2. Ⓨ Ⓝ

3. Ⓨ Ⓝ

4. Ⓨ Ⓝ

5. Ⓨ Ⓝ

6. Ⓨ Ⓝ

7. Ⓨ Ⓝ

8. Ⓨ Ⓝ

___ / 8
Total

NAME: _____ DATE: _____

DIRECTIONS Read and answer each question.

1. (Y)(N)

1. Write the missing punctuation in the sentence.

Youd be wrong if you think toilets are a recent invention.

2. (Y)(N)

2. Write the missing punctuation in the sentence.

Almost 3,000 years ago King Minos had a flushing toilet in Crete.

3. (Y)(N)

3. Circle the word that should be capitalized in the sentence.

4. (Y)(N)

A toilet was also found in the tomb of an ancient chinese king.

5. (Y)(N)

4. Underline the preposition in sentence A below.

5. Circle the prepositional phrase in sentence A below.

6. (Y)(N)

A The ancient Romans built sewer systems in the city.

7. (Y)(N)

6. Underline the article in sentence B below.

7. Circle the prepositional phrase in sentence B below.

8. (Y)(N)

B By the 1800s, people realized cleanliness was important.

___ / 8
Total

8. Circle the word below that is spelled correctly.

plumber   plummer   plumbur

NAME: _____ **DATE:** _____

DIRECTIONS Read and answer each question.

1. Write the missing punctuation in the sentence.

Whats the right thing to do when you are about to cough?

2. Write the missing punctuation in the sentence.

If you don't have a tissue do you cover your mouth with your hands?

3. Circle the word that should be capitalized in the sentence.

If you used to watch *Sesame street*, you know what to do.

4. Underline the helping verb in sentence A below.

5. Circle the preposition in sentence A below.

A Cold viruses can live for several hours.

6. Underline the verbs in sentence B below.

7. Circle the conjunction in sentence B below.

B Sneeze or cough into your elbow.

8. Circle the word below that is spelled correctly.

prescription

prescrition

prescirption

1. Ⓨ Ⓝ

2. Ⓨ Ⓝ

3. Ⓨ Ⓝ

4. Ⓨ Ⓝ

5. Ⓨ Ⓝ

6. Ⓨ Ⓝ

7. Ⓨ Ⓝ

8. Ⓨ Ⓝ

___ / 8
Total

NAME: _____ **DATE:** _____

DIRECTIONS Read and answer each question.

1. Y N

1. Write the missing punctuation in the sentence.

Would you like to know what is going to happen in your future

2. Y N

2. Write the missing punctuation in the sentence.

For thousands of years people have studied the sky for clues about the future.

3. Y N

3. Circle the word that should be capitalized in the sentence.

4. Y N

The word *horoscope* comes from greek words meaning "a look at the hours."

5. Y N

4. Underline the pronoun in sentence A below.

5. Circle the contraction in sentence A below.

6. Y N

A Scientists don't think you can tell the future.

7. Y N

6. Underline the possessive pronoun in sentence B below.

7. Circle the subject pronoun in sentence B below.

8. Y N

B However, you can have fun reading your horoscope.

___ / 8
Total

8. Circle the word below that is spelled correctly.

predictoin

prediction

perdiction

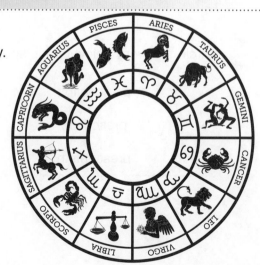

 #51170—180 Days of Language

NAME: _____ DATE: _____

DIRECTIONS Read and answer each question.

1. Write the missing punctuation in the sentence.

For many years you could see ghost ships in California.

2. Write the missing punctuation in the sentence.

Rusting U.S Navy ships, tied together floated in a bay near San Francisco.

3. Circle the word that should be capitalized in the sentence.

The ships, called the *ghost fleet*, were used during world War II.

4. Underline the helping verb in sentence A below.

5. Circle the proper noun in sentence A below.

A The ships were polluting Suisun Bay.

6. Underline the preposition in sentence B below.

7. Circle the helping verb in sentence B below.

B Most of the ships are being hauled away.

8. Circle the word below that is spelled correctly.

boyant   bouyant   buoyant

1. Ⓨ Ⓝ

2. Ⓨ Ⓝ

3. Ⓨ Ⓝ

4. Ⓨ Ⓝ

5. Ⓨ Ⓝ

6. Ⓨ Ⓝ

7. Ⓨ Ⓝ

8. Ⓨ Ⓝ

___ / 8
Total

NAME: _____ DATE: _____

SCORE

DIRECTIONS Read and answer each question.

1. Ⓨ Ⓝ

2. Ⓨ Ⓝ

3. Ⓨ Ⓝ

4. Ⓨ Ⓝ

5. Ⓨ Ⓝ

6. Ⓨ Ⓝ

7. Ⓨ Ⓝ

8. Ⓨ Ⓝ

___ / 8
Total

1. Write the missing punctuation in the sentence.

Most people, when there is an emergency dial 911.

2. Write the missing punctuation in the sentence.

Its comforting to know that help is on the way.

3. Circle the word that should be capitalized in the sentence.

An emergency medical technician, called an emt, will help.

4. Underline the adverb in sentence A below.

5. Circle the compound subject in sentence A below.

Ⓐ He or she may communicate directly with a doctor.

6. Underline the verbs in sentence B below.

7. Circle the adverb in sentence B below.

Ⓑ These people study hard to save lives.

8. Circle the word below that is spelled correctly.

ambulance

ambulence

ambullance

#51170—180 Days of Language

NAME: _____ DATE: _____

DIRECTIONS Read and answer each question.

1. Write the missing punctuation in the sentence.

Sarah Winchester, who inherited a fortune believed in ghosts.

1. Ⓨ Ⓝ

2. Write the missing punctuation in the sentence.

By 1862 she was depressed from the deaths of her daughter and husband.

2. Ⓨ Ⓝ

3. Ⓨ Ⓝ

3. Circle the word that should be capitalized in the sentence.

She decided to build a house in San josé, California.

4. Ⓨ Ⓝ

4. Underline the conjunction in sentence A below.

5. Ⓨ Ⓝ

5. Circle the contraction in sentence A below.

Ⓐ She thought she'd live forever if she kept building a house for ghosts.

6. Ⓨ Ⓝ

6. Underline the proper noun in sentence B below.

7. Ⓨ Ⓝ

7. Circle the helping verb in sentence B below.

Ⓑ The huge house is called the Winchester Mystery House.

8. Ⓨ Ⓝ

___ / 8
Total

8. Circle the word below that is spelled correctly.

basemeant

basment

basement

NAME: _____   **DATE:** _____

DIRECTIONS   Read and answer each question.

SCORE

1. Ⓨ Ⓝ

2. Ⓨ Ⓝ

3. Ⓨ Ⓝ

4. Ⓨ Ⓝ

5. Ⓨ Ⓝ

6. Ⓨ Ⓝ

7. Ⓨ Ⓝ

8. Ⓨ Ⓝ

___ / 8
Total

1. Write the missing punctuation in the sentence.

In 1929 no one realized just how bad times were going to get.

2. Write the missing punctuation in the sentence.

Many banks failed and people lost all their savings.

3. Circle the word that should be capitalized in the sentence.

The great Depression lasted more than ten years.

4. Underline the complete subject in sentence A below.

5. Circle the complete predicate in sentence A below.

Ⓐ People struggled to find jobs of any kind.

6. Underline the adverb in sentence B below.

7. Circle the adjectives in sentence B below.

Ⓑ New programs, set up by the government, slowly helped the country.

8. Circle the word below that is spelled correctly.

hadrship

hardchip

hardship

NAME: _____ DATE: _____

DIRECTIONS Read and answer each question.

1. Write the missing punctuation in the sentence.

Do you know how much a cup of gold, if flattened, could cover

1. Ⓨ Ⓝ

2. Write the missing punctuation in the sentence.

That gold, when flattened very thin could cover a football field.

2. Ⓨ Ⓝ

3. Ⓨ Ⓝ

3. Circle the word that should be capitalized in the sentence.

Experts think that only about 10 percent of the gold in california has been found.

4. Ⓨ Ⓝ

4. Underline the helping verb in sentence A below.

5. Ⓨ Ⓝ

5. Circle the articles in sentence A below.

Ⓐ A gold golf ball would weigh more than a brick.

6. Ⓨ Ⓝ

6. Underline the adverb in sentence B below.

7. Ⓨ Ⓝ

7. Circle the conjunction in sentence B below.

Ⓑ Gold can be melted down and made into new things.

8. Ⓨ Ⓝ

___ / 8
Total

8. Circle the word below that is spelled correctly.

precious

precoius

preciuos

NAME: _____ **DATE:** _____

DIRECTIONS Read and answer each question.

1. Ⓨ Ⓝ

1. Write the missing punctuation in the sentence.

If you live in the northern states it probably snows in the winter.

2. Ⓨ Ⓝ

2. Write the missing punctuation in the sentence.

Whats it like to have more than 100 inches of snow each winter?

3. Ⓨ Ⓝ

3. Circle the word that should be capitalized in the sentence.

4. Ⓨ Ⓝ

People in juneau, Alaska, have about that much snow every year.

5. Ⓨ Ⓝ

4. Underline the proper noun in sentence A below.

5. Circle the verb in sentence A below.

6. Ⓨ Ⓝ

Ⓐ In parts of Canada, people call soft, deep snow *mauja*.

7. Ⓨ Ⓝ

6. Underline the verb in sentence B below.

7. Circle the adjective in sentence B below.

8. Ⓨ Ⓝ

Ⓑ Eskimos call watery snow *mangokpok*.

___ / 8
Total

8. Circle the word below that is spelled correctly.

measure

meisure

meassure

NAME: _____ **DATE:** _____

DIRECTIONS Read and answer each question.

1. Write the missing punctuation in the sentence.

During World War II some men in Norway wanted to smuggle gold past the Nazis to a ship.

1. Ⓨ Ⓝ

2. Write the missing punctuation in the sentence.

Young Peter overhears his uncle talking to them and Peter gets an idea.

2. Ⓨ Ⓝ

3. Circle the word that should be capitalized in the sentence.

Peter tells uncle Victor that he and his friends can sneak the gold to the ship.

3. Ⓨ Ⓝ

4. Underline the verb in sentence A below.

4. Ⓨ Ⓝ

5. Circle the complete subject in sentence A below.

Ⓐ The children zip past the soldiers with gold on their sleds.

5. Ⓨ Ⓝ

6. Circle the title in sentence B below.

6. Ⓨ Ⓝ

7. Underline the pronoun in sentence B below.

Ⓑ You can read about this true story in <u>Snow Treasure</u> by Marie McSwigan.

7. Ⓨ Ⓝ

8. Ⓨ Ⓝ

8. Circle the word below that is spelled correctly.

invisable

invisible

invissible

___ / 8
Total

NAME: _____ **DATE:** _____

DIRECTIONS Read and answer each question.

1. Y N

1. Write the missing punctuation in the sentence.

Do you believe in sea monsters

2. Y N

2. Write the missing punctuation in the sentence.

If you saw a giant squid, youd believe sea monsters exist.

3. Y N

3. Circle the word that should be capitalized in the sentence.

4. Y N

This sea monster's name is *architeuthis dux*.

5. Y N

4. Underline the linking verb in sentence A below.

5. Circle the adjectives in sentence A below.

6. Y N

A This giant squid is sometimes longer than a school bus!

7. Y N

6. Underline the possessive pronoun in sentence B below.

7. Circle the linking verb in sentence B below.

8. Y N

B Its eyes are the size of hubcaps!

___ / 8
Total

8. Circle the word below that is spelled correctly.

tentacals

tenacles

tentacles

NAME: _____ **DATE:** _____

DIRECTIONS Read and answer each question.

1. Write the missing punctuation in the sentence.

Do you know what the words *taw aggie,* and *mibs* mean?

2. Write the missing punctuation in the sentence.

If you do you probably play marbles.

3. Circle the word that should be capitalized in the sentence.

Marbles have been found in the tombs of ancient egyptians.

4. Underline the linking verb in sentence A below.

5. Circle the nouns in sentence A below.

A An aggie is a marble made from a stone called agate.

6. Underline the adjective in sentence B below.

7. Circle the conjunction in sentence B below.

B Mibs and taw are names for different marbles.

8. Circle the word below that is spelled correctly.

hopskosh

hopskotch

hopscotch

1. Ⓨ Ⓝ

2. Ⓨ Ⓝ

3. Ⓨ Ⓝ

4. Ⓨ Ⓝ

5. Ⓨ Ⓝ

6. Ⓨ Ⓝ

7. Ⓨ Ⓝ

8. Ⓨ Ⓝ

___ / 8
Total

NAME: _____ **DATE:** _____

SCORE

1. Ⓨ Ⓝ

2. Ⓨ Ⓝ

3. Ⓨ Ⓝ

4. Ⓨ Ⓝ

5. Ⓨ Ⓝ

6. Ⓨ Ⓝ

7. Ⓨ Ⓝ

8. Ⓨ Ⓝ

____ / 8
Total

1. Write the missing punctuation in the sentence.

Do you do ten twenty, or thirty minutes of homework each night?

2. Write the missing punctuation in the sentence.

If you are in fifth grade you might be expected to do fifty minutes.

3. Circle the word that should be capitalized in the sentence.

In the United states, most students do about ten minutes per grade.

4. Underline the article in sentence A below.

5. Circle the prepositional phrase in sentence A below.

Ⓐ It helps to do your homework in a quiet place.

6. Underline the pronoun in sentence B below.

7. Circle the adjectives in sentence B below.

Ⓑ Take short breaks if you have a big project.

8. Circle the word below that is spelled correctly.

assigment

assignment

asignment

NAME: _____ DATE: _____

DIRECTIONS Read and answer each question.

1. Write the missing punctuation in the sentence.

Some people like to combine hiking rock climbing, and swimming.

1. Ⓨ Ⓝ

2. Write the missing punctuation in the sentence.

Called canyoneering, its an extreme sport.

2. Ⓨ Ⓝ

3. Ⓨ Ⓝ

3. Circle the word that should be capitalized in the sentence.

A flash flood killed 21 people while they were canyoneering in switzerland in 1997.

4. Ⓨ Ⓝ

4. Underline the adverb in sentence A below.

5. Ⓨ Ⓝ

5. Circle the helping verb in sentence A below.

6. Ⓨ Ⓝ

Ⓐ A heavy rainstorm can quickly cause a flash flood.

6. Underline the preposition in sentence B below.

7. Ⓨ Ⓝ

7. Circle the prepositional phrase in sentence B below.

8. Ⓨ Ⓝ

Ⓑ Escape is impossible when surrounded by high walls.

___ / 8
Total

8. Circle the word below that is spelled correctly.

tragady

tradgedy

tragedy

NAME: _____ **DATE:** _____

SCORE

1. (Y) (N)

2. (Y) (N)

3. (Y) (N)

4. (Y) (N)

5. (Y) (N)

6. (Y) (N)

7. (Y) (N)

8. (Y) (N)

____ / 8
Total

DIRECTIONS Read and answer each question.

1. Write the missing punctuation in the sentence.

Meet Nelly Bly a famous reporter who would do anything for a story.

2. Write the missing punctuation in the sentence.

In 1887 she pretends to be crazy.

3. Circle the word that should be capitalized in the sentence.

She is sent to Bellevue hospital for the insane.

4. Underline the verb in sentence A below.

5. Circle the contraction in sentence A below.

A After 10 days, she's rescued.

6. Underline the article in sentence B below.

7. Circle the pronouns in sentence B below.

B Through her reporting, she exposes the terrible treatment of women.

8. Circle the word below that is spelled correctly.

journelist

journalist

journallist

#51170—180 Days of Language © Shell Education

NAME: _____ **DATE:** _____

DIRECTIONS Read and answer each question.

1. Write the missing punctuation in the sentence.

During the Great Depression people moved as they looked for work.

1. Ⓨ Ⓝ

2. Write the missing punctuation in the sentence.

Many were from Oklahoma, Texas Arkansas, and Missouri.

2. Ⓨ Ⓝ

3. Ⓨ Ⓝ

3. Circle the word that should be capitalized in the sentence.

Families could pay $1 per week to live at Weedpatch camp in California.

4. Ⓨ Ⓝ

4. Underline the proper noun in sentence A below.

5. Ⓨ Ⓝ

5. Circle the prepositional phrase in sentence A below.

Ⓐ Leo B. Hart established a school for the children.

6. Ⓨ Ⓝ

6. Underline the conjunction in sentence B below.

7. Ⓨ Ⓝ

7. Circle the possessive pronoun in sentence B below.

Ⓑ The children could learn while their parents worked in the fields.

8. Ⓨ Ⓝ

8. Circle the word below that is spelled correctly.

hounorable

honurable

honorable

___ / 8
Total

NAME: _____ DATE: _____

SCORE

DIRECTIONS Read and answer each question.

1. Ⓨ Ⓝ

1. Write the missing punctuation in the sentence.

Many writers, such as Scott O'Dell may take nearly a year to write a book.

2. Ⓨ Ⓝ

2. Write the missing punctuation in the sentence.

O'Dell, who did research for several months then wrote for another six months.

3. Ⓨ Ⓝ

3. Circle the word that should be capitalized in the sentence.

He received the newbery Medal for <u>Island of the Blue Dolphins</u>.

4. Ⓨ Ⓝ

4. Underline the proper noun in sentence A below.

5. Circle the prepositional phrase in sentence A below.

5. Ⓨ Ⓝ

Ⓐ O'Dell likes writing books for children.

6. Ⓨ Ⓝ

6. Underline the plural noun in sentence B below.

7. Ⓨ Ⓝ

7. Circle the pronoun in sentence B below.

8. Ⓨ Ⓝ

Ⓑ He said that children know how to live through a story.

___ / 8
Total

8. Circle the word below that is spelled correctly.

optimism

optinism

optemism

#51170—180 Days of Language   © Shell Education

NAME: _____ **DATE:** _____

DIRECTIONS Read and answer each question.

1. Write the missing punctuation in the sentence.

Sojourner Truths birth name was Isabella Baumfree.

1. Ⓨ Ⓝ

2. Write the missing punctuation in the sentence.

Born in 1797 she was part of a slave family in upstate New York.

2. Ⓨ Ⓝ

3. Ⓨ Ⓝ

3. Circle the word that should be capitalized in the sentence.

Her second master, John neely, punished her often.

4. Ⓨ Ⓝ

4. Underline the conjunction in sentence A below.

5. Ⓨ Ⓝ

5. Circle the pronoun in sentence A below.

A During the Civil War, she preached about freedom and religion.

6. Ⓨ Ⓝ

6. Underline the preposition in sentence B below.

7. Ⓨ Ⓝ

7. Circle the verb in sentence B below.

B A famous painting shows her with President Abraham Lincoln.

8. Ⓨ Ⓝ

8. Circle the word below that is spelled correctly.

meaningfull

meeningful

meaningful

___ / 8
Total

NAME: _____ DATE: _____

DIRECTIONS Read and answer each question.

1. Write the missing punctuation in the sentence.

The first president, George Washington loved ice cream.

2. Write the missing punctuation in the sentence.

In May 1784 he got a machine for making ice cream.

3. Circle the word that should be capitalized in the sentence.

Mrs. martha Washington served ice cream at her parties.

4. Underline the proper noun in sentence A below.

5. Circle the possessive pronoun in sentence A below.

A There were many ice cream pots at his home, Mount Vernon.

6. Underline the verb in sentence B below.

7. Circle the complete subject in sentence B below.

B Washington spent $200 for ice cream one summer.

8. Circle the word below that is spelled correctly.

enjoyment

enjoiyment

enjoymeant

NAME: _____ **DATE:** _____

DIRECTIONS Read and answer each question.

1. Write the missing punctuation in the sentence.

In 1940 everyone thought that the only cartoonists were men.

1. Ⓨ Ⓝ

2. Write the missing punctuation in the sentence.

However one was actually a woman.

2. Ⓨ Ⓝ

3. Ⓨ Ⓝ

3. Circle the word that should be capitalized in the sentence.

Instead of using her real name, dalia Messick changed her name to Dale.

4. Ⓨ Ⓝ

4. Underline the proper noun in sentence A below.

5. Ⓨ Ⓝ

5. Circle the adjectives in sentence A below.

Ⓐ She created a glamorous reporter, Brenda Starr.

6. Ⓨ Ⓝ

6. Underline the conjunction in sentence B below.

7. Ⓨ Ⓝ

7. Circle the linking verb in sentence B below.

Ⓑ Dale and Brenda were both heroes!

8. Ⓨ Ⓝ

8. Circle the word below that is spelled correctly.

aceptable

acceptible

acceptable

___ / 8
Total

NAME: _____ DATE: _____

DIRECTIONS Read and answer each question.

1. Ⓨ Ⓝ

2. Ⓨ Ⓝ

3. Ⓨ Ⓝ

4. Ⓨ Ⓝ

5. Ⓨ Ⓝ

6. Ⓨ Ⓝ

7. Ⓨ Ⓝ

8. Ⓨ Ⓝ

___ / 8
Total

1. Write the missing punctuation in the sentence.

When the United States had its 100th birthday it got a big present.

2. Write the missing punctuation in the sentence.

The people of France wanting to help celebrate, sent America the Statue of Liberty.

3. Circle the word that should be capitalized in the sentence.

France had helped the country during the American revolution.

4. Underline the complete subject in sentence A below.

5. Circle the verb in sentence A below.

Ⓐ The statue came to America by ship.

6. Underline the helping verb in sentence B below.

7. Circle the conjunction in sentence B below.

Ⓑ It was packed in 214 crates and assembled here.

8. Circle the word below that is spelled correctly.

indipendence

independunce

independence

NAME: _____ **DATE:** _____

DIRECTIONS Read and answer each question.

1. Write the missing punctuation in the sentence.

Tatanka-Iyotanka, who lived from 1831 to 1890 was a Hunkpapa Lakota chief.

2. Write the missing punctuation in the sentence.

Known as Sitting Bull he was very courageous.

3. Circle the word that should be capitalized in the sentence.

Gold was discovered in the Black hills, a sacred area to many tribes.

4. Underline the conjunction in sentence A below.

5. Circle the proper nouns in sentence A below.

A Sitting Bull and Crazy Horse led warriors in a fight to save their land.

6. Underline the pronoun in sentence B below.

7. Circle the verbs in sentence B below.

B They defeated the U.S. troops led by George Armstrong Custer.

8. Circle the word below that is spelled correctly.

rebellious

rebelious

rebellous

1. Ⓨ Ⓝ

2. Ⓨ Ⓝ

3. Ⓨ Ⓝ

4. Ⓨ Ⓝ

5. Ⓨ Ⓝ

6. Ⓨ Ⓝ

7. Ⓨ Ⓝ

8. Ⓨ Ⓝ

___ / 8
Total

NAME: _____ **DATE:** _____

DIRECTIONS Read and answer each question.

1. (Y)(N)

2. (Y)(N)

3. (Y)(N)

4. (Y)(N)

5. (Y)(N)

6. (Y)(N)

7. (Y)(N)

8. (Y)(N)

___ / 8
Total

1. Write the missing punctuation in the sentence.

Leo Lionni was born in Amsterdam Holland.

2. Write the missing punctuation in the sentence.

After coming to the United States in 1931 he started a career in graphic design.

3. Circle the word that should be capitalized in the sentence.

You may have heard of some of his books, such as <u>Swimmy</u> or <u>frederick</u>.

4. Underline the possessive pronoun in sentence A below.

5. Circle the subject pronoun in sentence A below.

A He watched his grandchildren playing with scraps of paper.

6. Underline the prepositional phrase in sentence B below.

7. Circle the article in sentence B below.

B That gave him the idea for his book illustrations.

8. Circle the word below that is spelled correctly.

styel

style

stylle

NAME: _____ **DATE:** _____

DIRECTIONS Read and answer each question.

1. Write the missing punctuation in the sentence.

Have you ever needed help with spelling writing, or reading?

1. (Y)(N)

2. Write the missing punctuation in the sentence.

Its sometimes hard to get homework done.

2. (Y)(N)

3. (Y)(N)

3. Circle the word that should be capitalized in the sentence.

Todd strasser, a writer of many books, needed reading tutors.

4. (Y)(N)

4. Underline the linking verb in sentence A below.

5. (Y)(N)

5. Circle the possessive pronoun in sentence A below.

A "My reading comprehension was terrible," Todd said.

6. (Y)(N)

6. Underline the adverb in sentence B below.

7. (Y)(N)

7. Circle the speaker tag in sentence B below.

B "Writing is mostly rewriting," Todd added.

8. (Y)(N)

8. Circle the word below that is spelled correctly.

differant   different   diffirent

___ / 8
Total

NAME: _____   DATE: _____

1. Ⓨ Ⓝ

2. Ⓨ Ⓝ

3. Ⓨ Ⓝ

4. Ⓨ Ⓝ

5. Ⓨ Ⓝ

6. Ⓨ Ⓝ

7. Ⓨ Ⓝ

8. Ⓨ Ⓝ

___ / 8
Total

DIRECTIONS   Read and answer each question.

1. Write the missing punctuation in the sentence.

Martin Luther King Jr was born on January 15, 1929.

2. Write the missing punctuation in the sentence.

He had an older sister and a younger brother so he was the middle child.

3. Circle the word that should be capitalized in the sentence.

He grew up in Atlanta, georgia.

4. Underline the conjunction in sentence A below.

5. Circle the article in sentence A below.

Ⓐ   He became a famous preacher and civil rights leader.

6. Underline the linking verb in sentence B below.

7. Circle the possessive pronoun in sentence B below.

Ⓑ   His "I Have a Dream" speech is still famous.

8. Circle the word below that is spelled correctly.

tolerance

tolerence

tollerance

NAME: _____ **DATE:** _____

> **DIRECTIONS** Read and answer each question.

1. Write the missing punctuation in the sentence.

....

Do you know how much you should exercise each week

....

1. Ⓨ Ⓝ

2. Write the missing punctuation in the sentence.

....

Experts say kids should do exercises that strengthen muscles strengthen bones, and get you moving.

....

2. Ⓨ Ⓝ

3. Ⓨ Ⓝ

3. Circle the word that should be capitalized in the sentence.

....

try to do sixty minutes of exercise three times a week.

....

4. Ⓨ Ⓝ

4. Underline the helping verb in sentence A below.

5. Ⓨ Ⓝ

5. Circle the plural noun in sentence A below.

6. Ⓨ Ⓝ

Ⓐ You can play running games, jump rope, or ride your bike.

....

7. Ⓨ Ⓝ

6. Underline the prepositional phrase in sentence B below.

7. Circle the contraction in sentence B below.

8. Ⓨ Ⓝ

....

Ⓑ Choose something that's fun for you!

....

___ / 8
Total

8. Circle the word below that is spelled correctly.

....

movemant

movment

movement

....

NAME: _____ DATE: _____

DIRECTIONS Read and answer each question.

1. Ⓨ Ⓝ

1. Write the missing punctuation in the sentence.

Imagine having to escape Paris France on a bicycle.

2. Ⓨ Ⓝ

2. Write the missing punctuation in the sentence.

In 1940 Margret and Hans Rey took very little along when they fled the Nazis.

3. Ⓨ Ⓝ

3. Circle the word that should be capitalized in the sentence.

4. Ⓨ Ⓝ

They did take their book manuscripts, including <u>curious George</u>.

5. Ⓨ Ⓝ

4. Underline the adjectives in sentence A below.

5. Circle the contraction in sentence A below.

6. Ⓨ Ⓝ

Ⓐ The curious monkey wasn't called George at first.

7. Ⓨ Ⓝ

6. Underline the proper noun in sentence B below.

7. Circle the helping verb in sentence B below.

8. Ⓨ Ⓝ

Ⓑ He was called Fifi!

___ / 8
Total

8. Circle the word below that is spelled correctly.

trepadation

trepudation

trepidation

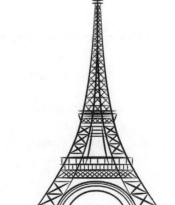

NAME: _____ DATE: _____

DIRECTIONS Read and answer each question.

1. Write the missing punctuation in the sentence.

"Hurry up We're going to be late!" said Washington.

2. Write the missing punctuation in the sentence.

It was June 10 the last day of fifth grade.

3. Circle the word that should be capitalized in the sentence.

Washington got an award for Most Improved reader.

4. Underline the prepositional phrase in sentence A below.

5. Circle the possessive noun in sentence A below.

A Washington's parents cheered for him.

6. Underline the prepositional phrase in sentence B below.

7. Circle the verb in sentence B below.

B They celebrated with pizza and lemonade.

8. Circle the word below that is spelled correctly.

garduation

gradaution

graduation

1. Ⓨ Ⓝ

2. Ⓨ Ⓝ

3. Ⓨ Ⓝ

4. Ⓨ Ⓝ

5. Ⓨ Ⓝ

6. Ⓨ Ⓝ

7. Ⓨ Ⓝ

8. Ⓨ Ⓝ

___ / 8
Total

NAME: _____ **DATE:** _____

DIRECTIONS Read and answer each question.

1. Write the missing punctuation in the sentence.

"Ouch " Rina said.

2. Write the missing punctuation in the sentence.

"Ive been bitten by a mosquito!" she exclaimed.

3. Circle the word that should be capitalized in the sentence.

Most mosquito bites are just annoying, but some spread the West nile virus.

4. Underline the complete subject in sentence A below.

5. Circle the helping verb in sentence A below.

Ⓐ That virus can make you feel worse than the flu.

6. Underline the verbs in sentence B below.

7. Circle the plural noun in sentence B below.

Ⓑ If there are a lot of mosquitos, stay inside.

8. Circle the word below that is spelled correctly.

niusance

nusance

nuisance

NAME: _____ **DATE:** _____

DIRECTIONS Read and answer each question.

1. Write the missing punctuation in the sentence.

Washington D.C. is the capital of the United States.

2. Write the missing punctuation in the sentence.

Theres plenty to see and do in the capital.

3. Circle the word that should be capitalized in the sentence.

The Smithsonian institution includes many museums.

4. Underline the proper noun in sentence A below.

5. Circle the plural noun in sentence A below.

A The museums and the National Zoo are free.

6. Underline the preposition in sentence B below.

7. Circle the plural nouns in sentence B below.

B You can see statues in the outdoor areas.

8. Circle the word below that is spelled correctly.

monoument

mounument

monument

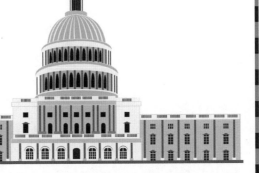

1. Ⓨ Ⓝ

2. Ⓨ Ⓝ

3. Ⓨ Ⓝ

4. Ⓨ Ⓝ

5. Ⓨ Ⓝ

6. Ⓨ Ⓝ

7. Ⓨ Ⓝ

8. Ⓨ Ⓝ

___ / 8
Total

NAME: _____ **DATE:** _____

SCORE

1. Ⓨ Ⓝ

2. Ⓨ Ⓝ

3. Ⓨ Ⓝ

4. Ⓨ Ⓝ

5. Ⓨ Ⓝ

6. Ⓨ Ⓝ

7. Ⓨ Ⓝ

8. Ⓨ Ⓝ

___ / 8
Total

DIRECTIONS Read and answer each question.

1. Write the missing punctuation in the sentence.

Theres an interesting thing happening in some schools in South Korea.

2. Write the missing punctuation in the sentence.

Some of the teachers are robots

3. Circle the word that should be capitalized in the sentence.

The robots are controlled by english teachers in another country.

4. Underline the verbs in sentence A below.

5. Circle the plural nouns in sentence A below.

Ⓐ The teachers can see and hear the children.

6. Underline the adjectives in sentence B below.

7. Circle the conjunction in sentence B below.

Ⓑ The robots give extra help, but they don't replace the teachers.

8. Circle the word below that is spelled correctly.

atendance

attendance

attendence

#51170—180 Days of Language
© Shell Education

NAME: _____ **DATE:** _____

DIRECTIONS Read and answer each question.

1. Write the missing punctuation in the sentence.

If you are called a Benedict Arnold that is an insult.

1. Ⓨ Ⓝ

2. Write the missing punctuation in the sentence.

During the Revolutionary War Arnold was thought to be a hero.

2. Ⓨ Ⓝ

3. Ⓨ Ⓝ

3. Circle the word that should be capitalized in the sentence.

However, in 1779 he decided to help the british.

4. Ⓨ Ⓝ

4. Underline the conjunction in sentence A below.

5. Ⓨ Ⓝ

5. Circle the complete subject in sentence A below.

Ⓐ Arnold planned to betray our country for money and power.

6. Ⓨ Ⓝ

6. Underline the verb in sentence B below.

7. Ⓨ Ⓝ

7. Circle the prepositional phrase in sentence B below.

Ⓑ Now, that name stands for traitor.

8. Ⓨ Ⓝ

8. Circle the word below that is spelled correctly.

deceitful

deceitfull

deceetful

___ / 8
Total

NAME: _____ DATE: _____

DIRECTIONS Read and answer each question.

1. Ⓨ Ⓝ

2. Ⓨ Ⓝ

3. Ⓨ Ⓝ

4. Ⓨ Ⓝ

5. Ⓨ Ⓝ

6. Ⓨ Ⓝ

7. Ⓨ Ⓝ

8. Ⓨ Ⓝ

___ / 8
Total

1. Write the missing punctuation in the sentence.

Do you know where the coldest driest, and windiest place is on Earth?

2. Write the missing punctuation in the sentence.

If you said *Antarctica* you would be correct.

3. Circle the word that should be capitalized in the sentence.

One of the most famous polar explorers is roald Amundsen.

4. Underline the adjectives in sentence A below.

5. Circle the linking verb in sentence A below.

Ⓐ He was the first man to go to the South Pole.

6. Underline the complete subject in sentence B below.

7. Circle the adjectives in sentence B below.

Ⓑ He used strong sled dogs for his journey to the South Pole.

8. Circle the word below that is spelled correctly.

contnent

contenent

continent

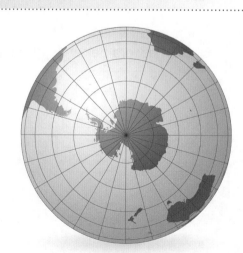

NAME: _____ DATE: _____

DIRECTIONS Read and answer each question.

1. Write the missing punctuation in the sentence.

In the early 1970s many people began to use a new tool.

1. Y N

2. Write the missing punctuation in the sentence.

This small powerful calculator fit in a pocket.

2. Y N

3. Y N

3. Circle the word that should be capitalized in the sentence.

The chinese invented a calculator, too.

4. Y N

4. Underline the complete predicate in sentence A below.

5. Y N

5. Circle the possessive pronoun in sentence A below.

A Their abacus has been used for thousands of years.

6. Y N

6. Underline the article in sentence B below.

7. Y N

7. Circle the contraction in sentence B below.

B You can compute with it, and you don't need a battery!

8. Y N

8. Circle the word below that is spelled correctly.

acurate

accurrate

accurate

___ / 8
Total

NAME: _____ **DATE:** _____

DIRECTIONS Read and answer each question.

1. Write the missing punctuation in the sentence.

On November 5, 1872 several women got into a lot of trouble.

2. Write the missing punctuation in the sentence.

Theyd go down in history just for trying to vote.

3. Circle the word that should be capitalized in the sentence.

Susan B. anthony led the group of women.

4. Underline the conjunction in sentence A below.

5. Circle the pronoun in sentence A below.

Ⓐ She was arrested and tried for the crime of voting without having that right.

6. Underline the verbs in sentence B below.

7. Circle the pronoun in sentence B below.

Ⓑ Anthony lost the trial, but she never paid the fine!

8. Circle the word below that is spelled correctly.

adjourn

adjorn

ajourn

NAME: _____ **DATE:** _____

DIRECTIONS Read and answer each question.

1. Write the missing punctuation in the sentence.

Have you ever been entertained by a mime

1. Ⓨ Ⓝ

2. Write the missing punctuation in the sentence.

A mime tells a story using gestures movement, and expressions.

2. Ⓨ Ⓝ

3. Ⓨ Ⓝ

3. Circle the word that should be capitalized in the sentence.

Marcel Marceau studied acting in paris, France.

4. Ⓨ Ⓝ

4. Underline the proper noun in sentence A below.

5. Ⓨ Ⓝ

5. Circle the pronoun in sentence A below.

Ⓐ He created a clown character called Bip.

6. Ⓨ Ⓝ

6. Underline the adjectives in sentence B below.

7. Ⓨ Ⓝ

7. Circle the preposition in sentence B below.

Ⓑ As Bip, Marceau used a floppy hat with a flower.

8. Ⓨ Ⓝ

8. Circle the word below that is spelled correctly.

appearence

apearance

appearance

___ / 8
Total

NAME: _____ DATE: _____

DIRECTIONS Read and answer each question.

SCORE

1. (Y) (N)

1. Write the missing punctuation in the sentence.

One legend tells about a monster with a long neck a bird head, and a booming voice.

2. (Y) (N)

2. Write the missing punctuation in the sentence.

3. (Y) (N)

Called a *bunyip* it is thought to eat people when it can't find other food.

3. Circle the word that should be capitalized in the sentence.

4. (Y) (N)

It is believed to live in swamps, rivers, or lakes in the australian outback.

5. (Y) (N)

4. Underline the plural nouns in sentence A below.

6. (Y) (N)

5. Circle the prepositional phrase in sentence A below.

A Legend says bunyips also cause disease in people.

7. (Y) (N)

6. Underline the conjunction in sentence B below.

8. (Y) (N)

7. Circle the adjective in sentence B below.

B Its name means "evil spirit" or "humbug."

___ / 8
Total

8. Circle the word below that is spelled correctly.

annoying   anoying   annoiying

NAME: _____ **DATE:** _____

DIRECTIONS Read and answer each question.

1. Write the missing punctuation in the sentence.

Squirrels, which live in most countries are rodents.

1. (Y)(N)

2. Write the missing punctuation in the sentence.

At just five inches long, its hard to spot the African pygmy squirrel.

2. (Y)(N)

3. (Y)(N)

3. Circle the word that should be capitalized in the sentence.

The indian giant squirrel is three feet long!

4. (Y)(N)

4. Underline the complete subject in sentence A below.

5. (Y)(N)

5. Circle the possessive pronoun in sentence A below.

A Their four front teeth never stop growing.

6. (Y)(N)

6. Underline the conjunction in sentence B below.

7. (Y)(N)

7. Circle the verb in sentence B below.

B They eat nuts, berries, bark, eggs, and flowers.

8. (Y)(N)

___ / 8
Total

8. Circle the word below that is spelled correctly.

chipmonk

chipmunk

chipmounk

NAME: _____ DATE: _____

DIRECTIONS Read and answer each question.

1. (Y)(N)

1. Write the missing punctuation in the sentence.

For many years December 17 was a special day in ancient Rome.

2. (Y)(N)

2. Write the missing punctuation in the sentence.

There was a big festival which they called *Saturnalia*.

3. (Y)(N)

3. Circle the word that should be capitalized in the sentence.

4. (Y)(N)

It was held in honor of the god saturn, whom they worshipped.

5. (Y)(N)

4. Underline the adjective in sentence A below.

5. Circle the verb in sentence A below.

6. (Y)(N)

A Men dressed in colorful clothes instead of togas.

7. (Y)(N)

6. Underline the adjective in sentence B below.

7. Circle the possessive pronoun in sentence B below.

8. (Y)(N)

B Rich people served their slaves at banquets.

___ / 8
Total

8. Circle the word below that is spelled correctly.

costume

coustume

costoum

NAME: _____ **DATE:** _____

DIRECTIONS Read and answer each question.

1. Write the missing punctuation in the sentence.

Some of Gary Paulsen's first jobs were a truck driver a carpenter, and a teacher.

1. Ⓨ Ⓝ

2. Write the missing punctuation in the sentence.

But he became famous for writing childrens books.

2. Ⓨ Ⓝ

3. Ⓨ Ⓝ

3. Circle the word that should be capitalized in the sentence.

Paulsen also completed the Iditarod Trail Sled Dog Race in alaska.

4. Ⓨ Ⓝ

4. Underline the verb in sentence A below.

5. Ⓨ Ⓝ

5. Circle the adverb in sentence A below.

A He often writes about dogs in his books.

6. Ⓨ Ⓝ

6. Underline the plural noun in sentence B below.

7. Ⓨ Ⓝ

7. Circle the possessive pronoun in sentence B below.

B Paulsen says that he has lived all of his stories.

8. Ⓨ Ⓝ

8. Circle the word below that is spelled correctly.

exciting

ekciting

exicting

___ / 8
Total

NAME: _____ DATE: _____

DIRECTIONS Read and answer each question.

1. (Y)(N)

2. (Y)(N)

3. (Y)(N)

4. (Y)(N)

5. (Y)(N)

6. (Y)(N)

7. (Y)(N)

8. (Y)(N)

___ / 8
Total

1. Write the missing punctuation in the sentence.

George de Mestral, an engineer liked to hike with his dog.

2. Write the missing punctuation in the sentence.

One day, he noticed cockleburs stuck in his dogs fur.

3. Circle the word that should be capitalized in the sentence.

That gave mr. de Mestral an idea.

4. Underline the plural noun in sentence A below.

5. Circle the pronoun in sentence A below.

A He used a microscope and saw how the cockleburs hooked onto the fur.

6. Underline the verb in sentence B below.

7. Circle the complete subject in sentence B below.

B That discovery resulted in the creation of velcro.

8. Circle the word below that is spelled correctly.

acident

accident

acciddent

NAME: _____ DATE: _____

DIRECTIONS Read and answer each question.

1. Write the missing punctuation in the sentence.

Have you ever watched wheelchair basketball

1. Ⓨ Ⓝ

2. Write the missing punctuation in the sentence.

People in wheelchairs can do many sports, such as golf tennis, and skiing.

2. Ⓨ Ⓝ

3. Ⓨ Ⓝ

3. Circle the word that should be capitalized in the sentence.

Wheelchair athletics began with injured World war II veterans.

4. Ⓨ Ⓝ

4. Underline the linking verb in sentence A below.

5. Ⓨ Ⓝ

5. Circle the article in sentence A below.

A The games are exciting and fun to watch.

6. Ⓨ Ⓝ

6. Underline the verb in sentence B below.

7. Ⓨ Ⓝ

7. Circle the proper noun in sentence B below.

B Top athletes compete in the Paralympics games.

8. Ⓨ Ⓝ

8. Circle the word below that is spelled correctly.

accessable

acessible

accessible

___ / 8
Total

NAME: _____ **DATE:** _____

DIRECTIONS Read and answer each question.

SCORE

1. Y N

1. Write the missing punctuation in the sentence.

In 1913 thousands of children read the book <u>Pollyanna</u>.

2. Y N

2. Write the missing punctuation in the sentence.

Pollyanna an orphan, has to live with her aunt.

3. Y N

3. Circle the word that should be capitalized in the sentence.

Although she is rich, aunt Polly is strict.

4. Y N

4. Underline the adverb in sentence A below.

5. Y N

5. Circle the proper noun in sentence A below.

6. Y N

A Pollyanna is always cheerful, even when punished.

7. Y N

6. Underline the article in sentence B below.

7. Circle the conjunction in sentence B below.

8. Y N

B When someone calls you a Pollyanna, smile and say "Thanks!"

___ / 8
Total

8. Circle the word below that is spelled correctly.

optimist   optimest   optimits

NAME: _____ **DATE:** _____

DIRECTIONS Read and answer each question.

1. Write the missing punctuation in the sentence.

On June 22, 1947, it began to rain in Holt Missouri.

1. Ⓨ Ⓝ

2. Write the missing punctuation in the sentence.

For 42 minutes it poured and poured!

2. Ⓨ Ⓝ

3. Ⓨ Ⓝ

3. Circle the word that should be capitalized in the sentence.

The rain filled the Missouri river.

4. Ⓨ Ⓝ

4. Underline the verb in sentence A below.

5. Ⓨ Ⓝ

5. Circle the prepositions in sentence A below.

Ⓐ Twelve inches of rain fell in 42 minutes.

6. Ⓨ Ⓝ

6. Underline the preposition in sentence B below.

7. Ⓨ Ⓝ

7. Circle the prepositional phrase in sentence B below.

Ⓑ The Holt storm set a world record for rainfall.

8. Ⓨ Ⓝ

8. Circle the word below that is spelled correctly.

umberlla

umbrela

umbrella

___ / 8
Total

NAME: _____ DATE: _____

DIRECTIONS Read and answer each question.

1. Ⓨ Ⓝ

2. Ⓨ Ⓝ

3. Ⓨ Ⓝ

4. Ⓨ Ⓝ

5. Ⓨ Ⓝ

6. Ⓨ Ⓝ

7. Ⓨ Ⓝ

8. Ⓨ Ⓝ

___ / 8
Total

1. Write the missing punctuation in the sentence.

During the Civil War Clara Barton wanted to help the wounded.

2. Write the missing punctuation in the sentence.

However women were not allowed to work in hospitals or on the battlefield.

3. Circle the word that should be capitalized in the sentence.

She wouldn't give up and was known as the Angel of the battlefield.

4. Underline the proper nouns in sentence A below.

5. Circle the verb in sentence A below.

Ⓐ After the war, she learned about the Red Cross in Europe.

6. Underline the preposition in sentence B below.

7. Circle the proper nouns in sentence B below.

Ⓑ Barton ran the American National Red Cross for 22 years.

8. Circle the word below that is spelled correctly.

senseble

sensable

sensible

NAME: _____ **DATE:** _____

DIRECTIONS Read and answer each question.

SCORE

1. Write the missing punctuation in the sentence.

If you had to name a new flower how would you choose a name?

1. Ⓨ Ⓝ

2. Write the missing punctuation in the sentence.

Would you call it *blazing star candytuft*, or *cowslip*?

2. Ⓨ Ⓝ

3. Ⓨ Ⓝ

3. Circle the words that should be capitalized in the sentence.

Those names are all used, along with *drumstick*, *lobster claw,* and *queen anne's lace*.

4. Ⓨ Ⓝ

5. Ⓨ Ⓝ

4. Underline the adjectives in sentence A below.

5. Circle the helping verb in sentence A below.

6. Ⓨ Ⓝ

A Some flowers are named after a person.

7. Ⓨ Ⓝ

6. Underline the plural noun in sentence B below.

7. Circle the possessive noun in sentence B below.

8. Ⓨ Ⓝ

B Other names give a clue about a flower's appearance.

____ / 8
Total

8. Circle the word below that is spelled correctly.

varible

variable

varable

NAME: _____ **DATE:** _____

DIRECTIONS Read and answer each question.

1. Ⓨ Ⓝ

1. Write the missing punctuation in the sentence.

If you have a fever, aches chills, and a cough, you may have the flu.

2. Ⓨ Ⓝ

2. Write the missing punctuation in the sentence.

The word *flu* is short for *influenza* and it can make you very sick.

3. Ⓨ Ⓝ

3. Circle the word that should be capitalized in the sentence.

4. Ⓨ Ⓝ

The Centers for Disease Control and prevention keep track of the flu.

5. Ⓨ Ⓝ

4. Underline the adverb in sentence A below.

5. Circle the verb in sentence A below.

6. Ⓨ Ⓝ

A   People often get flu shots.

7. Ⓨ Ⓝ

6. Underline the article in sentence B below.

7. Circle the possessive pronoun in sentence B below.

8. Ⓨ Ⓝ

B   You can help avoid the flu by washing your hands often.

___ / 8
Total

8. Circle the word below that is spelled correctly.

unbearible

unbearable

unbareable

NAME: _____ **DATE:** _____

DIRECTIONS Read and answer each question.

1. Write the missing punctuation in the sentence.

The Bermuda Triangle has been a mysterious area for many years

2. Write the missing punctuation in the sentence.

Legend claims that many planes ships, and people have disappeared there.

3. Circle the word that should be capitalized in the sentence.

It is in the western part of the Atlantic ocean.

4. Underline the adjective that modifies *place* in sentence A below.

5. Circle the contraction in sentence A below.

A Some people think it's a dangerous place.

6. Underline the verb in sentence B below.

7. Circle the preposition in sentence B below.

B However, any ocean can be dangerous for people.

8. Circle the word below that is spelled correctly.

imposible

impossible

impossable

1. Ⓨ Ⓝ

2. Ⓨ Ⓝ

3. Ⓨ Ⓝ

4. Ⓨ Ⓝ

5. Ⓨ Ⓝ

6. Ⓨ Ⓝ

7. Ⓨ Ⓝ

8. Ⓨ Ⓝ

___ / 8
Total

NAME: _____ **DATE:** _____

DIRECTIONS Read and answer each question.

1. (Y)(N)

1. Write the missing punctuation in the sentence.

When the circus came to town it was very exciting.

2. (Y)(N)

2. Write the missing punctuation in the sentence.

There was a parade of animals and a band was pulled in a wagon.

3. (Y)(N)

3. Circle the word that should be capitalized in the sentence.

Circus owners, such as P. T. barnum, wanted to attract attention.

4. (Y)(N)

4. Underline the adverb in sentence A below.

5. (Y)(N)

5. Circle the complete subject in sentence A below.

6. (Y)(N)

A Politicians also started using "bandwagons" to get attention.

7. (Y)(N)

6. Underline the contraction in sentence B below.

7. Circle the verbs in sentence B below.

8. (Y)(N)

B If you join a group or a cause, you're jumping on the bandwagon.

___ / 8
Total

8. Circle the word below that is spelled correctly.

meaningful

meaningfull

meaningfule

NAME: _____ DATE: _____

DIRECTIONS Read and answer each question.

1. Write the missing punctuation in the sentence.

When times are hard many people lose their homes.

1. Ⓨ Ⓝ

2. Write the missing punctuation in the sentence.

Families may move in with relatives or they may live in shelters.

2. Ⓨ Ⓝ

3. Ⓨ Ⓝ

3. Circle the word that should be capitalized in the sentence.

Some people get help from the United states government.

4. Ⓨ Ⓝ

4. Underline the conjunction in sentence A below.

5. Ⓨ Ⓝ

5. Circle the possessive pronoun in sentence A below.

6. Ⓨ Ⓝ

Ⓐ Even some pets lose their homes or families.

6. Underline the article in sentence B below.

7. Ⓨ Ⓝ

7. Circle the adverb in sentence B below.

8. Ⓨ Ⓝ

Ⓑ The animal-shelter workers try hard to find new homes for them.

8. Circle the word below that is spelled correctly.

penneless

pennyless

penniless

___ / 8
Total

NAME: _____ DATE: _____

Read and answer each question.

SCORE

1. Ⓨ Ⓝ

1. Write the missing punctuation in the sentence.

Has someone ever said to you that a watched pot never boils

2. Ⓨ Ⓝ

2. Write the missing punctuation in the sentence.

Youve been learning about time since you were born.

3. Ⓨ Ⓝ

3. Circle the word that should be capitalized in the sentence.

A researcher named Jennifer coull says that time drags when we are bored.

4. Ⓨ Ⓝ

4. Underline the adjectives in sentence A below.

5. Ⓨ Ⓝ

5. Circle the pronoun in sentence A below.

6. Ⓨ Ⓝ

A Time flies when we are happy or excited.

7. Ⓨ Ⓝ

6. Underline the compound word in sentence B below.

7. Circle the adverb in sentence B below.

8. Ⓨ Ⓝ

B If you want time to pass quickly, do something fun.

___ / 8
Total

8. Circle the word below that is spelled correctly.

inevatable

inevitible

inevitible

NAME: _____ DATE: _____

DIRECTIONS Read and answer each question.

1. Write the missing punctuation in the sentence.

If you were from China it was hard to come to America after 1882.

1. Ⓨ Ⓝ

2. Write the missing punctuation in the sentence.

By then the Chinese Exclusion Act of 1882 limited the people who could enter from China.

2. Ⓨ Ⓝ

3. Ⓨ Ⓝ

3. Circle the word that should be capitalized in the sentence.

Immigrants were held on Angel island near San Francisco for weeks or more.

4. Ⓨ Ⓝ

4. Underline the prepositional phrases in sentence A below.

5. Circle the plural noun in sentence A below.

5. Ⓨ Ⓝ

6. Ⓨ Ⓝ

A They had to prove they had relatives in America.

7. Ⓨ Ⓝ

6. Underline the helping verb in sentence B below.

7. Circle the adjectives in sentence B below.

8. Ⓨ Ⓝ

B Some people were kept on the island for a year.

___ / 8
Total

8. Circle the word below that is spelled correctly.

elegible   eligable   eligible

NAME: _____ DATE: _____

SCORE

1. (Y) (N)

2. (Y) (N)

3. (Y) (N)

4. (Y) (N)

5. (Y) (N)

6. (Y) (N)

7. (Y) (N)

8. (Y) (N)

___ / 8
Total

DIRECTIONS Read and answer each question.

1. Write the missing punctuation in the sentence.

Do you have a favorite musical group

2. Write the missing punctuation in the sentence.

If you grew up in the 1960s it might have been the Beatles.

3. Circle the word that should be capitalized in the sentence.

They started out by performing in liverpool, England.

4. Underline the preposition in sentence A below.

5. Circle the verb in sentence A below.

A They "invaded" the United States in 1964.

6. Underline the preposition in sentence B below.

7. Circle the proper nouns in sentence B below.

B The adoration for the Beatles was called *Beatlemania*.

8. Circle the word below that is spelled correctly.

fathful

faithful

faithfull

NAME: _____ DATE: _____

DIRECTIONS Read and answer each question.

1. Write the missing punctuation in the sentence.

For more than 50 years people have known about James Bond.

2. Write the missing punctuation in the sentence.

In addition to reading books they have watched movies about this spy.

3. Circle the word that should be capitalized in the sentence.

Ian fleming wrote twelve novels about Bond.

4. Underline the plural nouns in sentence A below.

5. Circle the possessive pronoun in sentence A below.

A Fleming based his stories on secret agents he met during World War II.

6. Underline the complete subject in sentence B below.

7. Circle the helping verb in sentence B below.

B Actors have portrayed Bond in more than 20 movies.

8. Circle the word below that is spelled correctly.

apparent   apparant   apparrent

1. Ⓨ Ⓝ

2. Ⓨ Ⓝ

3. Ⓨ Ⓝ

4. Ⓨ Ⓝ

5. Ⓨ Ⓝ

6. Ⓨ Ⓝ

7. Ⓨ Ⓝ

8. Ⓨ Ⓝ

___ / 8
Total

NAME: _____   DATE: _____

DIRECTIONS   Read and answer each question.

1. (Y)(N)

1. Write the missing punctuation in the sentence.

On November 14, 1963 something amazing happened.

2. (Y)(N)

2. Write the missing punctuation in the sentence.

While scientists watched an island was born.

3. (Y)(N)

4. (Y)(N)

3. Circle the word that should be capitalized in the sentence.

It happened in the north Atlantic near Iceland.

5. (Y)(N)

4. Underline the conjunction in sentence A below.

5. Circle the adjectives in sentence A below.

6. (Y)(N)

A An underwater volcano erupted, and the sea turned brown.

7. (Y)(N)

6. Underline the prepositional phrase in sentence B below.

7. Circle the helping verb in sentence B below.

8. (Y)(N)

B By the next night, a new island was born.

___ / 8
Total

8. Circle the word below that is spelled correctly.

unexpected

unexpeted

unexspected

NAME: _____ **DATE:** _____

DIRECTIONS Read and answer each question.

1. Write the missing punctuation in the sentence.

Each year avalanches take about 150 lives.

2. Write the missing punctuation in the sentence.

Its rare when a person survives after 15 minutes of being buried in an avalance.

3. Circle the word that should be capitalized in the sentence.

Rescue teams often use german shepherds when searching for people.

4. Underline the complete subject in sentence A below.

5. Circle the possessive pronoun in sentence A below.

A These dogs follow their noses!

6. Underline the prepositional phrase in sentence B below.

7. Circle the pronoun in sentence B below.

B They have an incredible sense of smell.

8. Circle the word below that is spelled correctly.

predicament

prediciment

predicameant

1. Ⓨ Ⓝ

2. Ⓨ Ⓝ

3. Ⓨ Ⓝ

4. Ⓨ Ⓝ

5. Ⓨ Ⓝ

6. Ⓨ Ⓝ

7. Ⓨ Ⓝ

8. Ⓨ Ⓝ

___ / 8
Total

NAME: _____ DATE: _____

1. Ⓨ Ⓝ

2. Ⓨ Ⓝ

3. Ⓨ Ⓝ

4. Ⓨ Ⓝ

5. Ⓨ Ⓝ

6. Ⓨ Ⓝ

7. Ⓨ Ⓝ

8. Ⓨ Ⓝ

___ / 8
Total

DIRECTIONS Read and answer each question.

1. Write the missing punctuation in the sentence.

You might greet a friend with a high five a hug, or a kiss.

2. Write the missing punctuation in the sentence.

Years ago your rank determined how you kissed a person.

3. Circle the word that should be capitalized in the sentence.

During the Middle ages in Europe, you'd kiss people below you on the hand.

4. Underline the prepositional phrase in sentence A below.

5. Circle the contraction in sentence A below.

A You'd kiss those higher than you on the knee.

6. Underline the helping verb in sentence B below.

7. Circle the adjectives in sentence B below.

B Religious leaders were kissed on the foot.

8. Circle the word below that is spelled correctly.

respectible   respectable   respectabile

NAME: _____ **DATE:** _____

DIRECTIONS Read and answer each question.

1. Write the missing punctuation in the sentence.

In 1963 there was a lot of conflict over civil rights.

1. Ⓨ Ⓝ

2. Write the missing punctuation in the sentence.

Many businesses clubs, and schools refused entry to African Americans.

2. Ⓨ Ⓝ

3. Ⓨ Ⓝ

3. Circle the word that should be capitalized in the sentence.

A bomb was set off in a church in birmingham, Alabama.

4. Ⓨ Ⓝ

4. Underline the prepositional phrase in sentence A below.

5. Ⓨ Ⓝ

5. Circle the helping verb in sentence A below.

Ⓐ Four young girls were killed in the blast.

6. Ⓨ Ⓝ

6. Circle the book title in sentence B below.

7. Ⓨ Ⓝ

7. Underline the pronoun in sentence B below.

Ⓑ You can read about this time in <u>The Watsons Go to Birmingham—1963</u> by Christopher Paul Curtis.

8. Ⓨ Ⓝ

___ / 8
Total

8. Circle the word below that is spelled correctly.

horrible

horruble

horible

NAME: _____ **DATE:** _____

DIRECTIONS Read and answer each question.

1. Ⓨ Ⓝ

1. Write the missing punctuation in the sentence.

It was a special night in Hollywood on February 29 1940.

2. Ⓨ Ⓝ

2. Write the missing punctuation in the sentence.

Hattie McDaniel, who was African American won an Academy Award.

3. Ⓨ Ⓝ

3. Circle the word that should be capitalized in the sentence.

She won it for her role in the movie *Gone with the wind*.

4. Ⓨ Ⓝ

4. Underline the prepositional phrase in sentence A below.

5. Ⓨ Ⓝ

5. Circle the adjectives in sentence A below.

6. Ⓨ Ⓝ

Ⓐ She was the first African American to win an Oscar.

7. Ⓨ Ⓝ

6. Underline the proper nouns in sentence B below.

7. Circle the verb in sentence B below.

8. Ⓨ Ⓝ

Ⓑ Hattie McDaniel died on October 26, 1952.

___ / 8
Total

8. Circle the word below that is spelled correctly.

seggregation

segregation

segrigation

#51170—180 Days of Language

NAME: _____ **DATE:** _____

DIRECTIONS Read and answer each question.

1. Write the missing punctuation in the sentence.

In medieval Europe some young men were trained to become soldiers.

2. Write the missing punctuation in the sentence.

They were trained in using weapons handling horses, and appropriate behavior.

3. Circle the word that should be capitalized in the sentence.

The code of chivalry, which is about honor, comes from the french word for horse—*cheval.*

4. Underline the helping verb in sentence A below.

5. Circle the prepositional phrase in sentence A below.

A Called knights, they were trained in royal courts.

6. Underline the complete predicate in sentence B below.

7. Circle the adjectives in sentence B below.

B Successful knights could become wealthy.

8. Circle the word below that is spelled correctly.

obedience

obedeince

obediance

1. Ⓨ Ⓝ

2. Ⓨ Ⓝ

3. Ⓨ Ⓝ

4. Ⓨ Ⓝ

5. Ⓨ Ⓝ

6. Ⓨ Ⓝ

7. Ⓨ Ⓝ

8. Ⓨ Ⓝ

___ / 8
Total

NAME: _____ **DATE:** _____

DIRECTIONS Read and answer each question.

1. Y N

1. Write the missing punctuation in the sentence.

If you got married in Rome long ago some practices would be similar to now.

2. Y N

2. Write the missing punctuation in the sentence.

Youd probably feed your spouse a piece of food.

3. Y N

3. Circle the word that should be capitalized in the sentence.

During the period of the Roman empire, the bride wore a wedding veil.

4. Y N

4. Underline the proper noun in sentence A below.

5. Y N

5. Circle the adjectives in sentence A below.

A The Romans believed the veil kept evil spirits away.

6. Y N

6. Underline the preposition in sentence B below.

7. Y N

7. Circle the prepositional phrase in sentence B below.

B Married women wore their wedding rings on their thumbs.

8. Y N

___ / 8
Total

8. Circle the word below that is spelled correctly.

elegent

elegant

elegeant

NAME: _____ **DATE:** _____

DIRECTIONS Read and answer each question.

SCORE

1. Write the missing punctuation in the sentence.

For decades the most valuable baseball cards were of Honus Wagner.

1. Ⓨ Ⓝ

2. Write the missing punctuation in the sentence.

Wagners cards were sold with cigarette packs.

2. Ⓨ Ⓝ

3. Ⓨ Ⓝ

3. Circle the word that should be capitalized in the sentence.

They were issued by the American Tobacco company.

4. Ⓨ Ⓝ

4. Underline the pronouns in sentence A below.

5. Ⓨ Ⓝ

5. Circle the proper noun in sentence A below.

A Wagner stopped their sale, perhaps because he opposed smoking.

6. Ⓨ Ⓝ

6. Underline the possessive pronoun in sentence B below.

7. Ⓨ Ⓝ

7. Circle the plural noun in sentence B below.

B One of his cards sold for more than $2,000,000!

8. Ⓨ Ⓝ

8. Circle the word below that is spelled correctly.

distribute

distributte

distribbute

___ / 8
Total

NAME: _____ **DATE:** _____

SCORE

1. Ⓨ Ⓝ

2. Ⓨ Ⓝ

3. Ⓨ Ⓝ

4. Ⓨ Ⓝ

5. Ⓨ Ⓝ

6. Ⓨ Ⓝ

7. Ⓨ Ⓝ

8. Ⓨ Ⓝ

___ / 8
Total

1. Write the missing punctuation in the sentence.

Have you ever really wanted a certain toy pair of shoes, or game?

2. Write the missing punctuation in the sentence.

Youre not the first person to follow a fad.

3. Circle the word that should be capitalized in the sentence.

One goofy fad dates back to the 1400s in europe.

4. Underline the verb in sentence A below.

5. Circle the complete subject in sentence A below.

A Men wore shoes with long, pointed toes.

6. Underline the helping verb in sentence B below.

7. Circle the conjunction in sentence B below.

B Some were stuffed with straw and shaped like lion claws!

8. Circle the word below that is spelled correctly.

curious

currious

curiuos

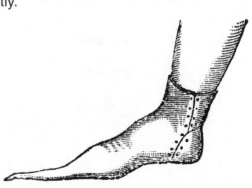

NAME: _____ **DATE:** _____

DIRECTIONS Read and answer each question.

1. Write the missing punctuation in the sentence.

Once you hear a group of howler monkeys you'll never forget it.

1. Ⓨ Ⓝ

2. Write the missing punctuation in the sentence.

Theyre so loud that you can hear them more than a mile away!

2. Ⓨ Ⓝ

3. Ⓨ Ⓝ

3. Circle the word that should be capitalized in the sentence.

If you want to hear them, visit South America or central America.

4. Ⓨ Ⓝ

4. Underline the verb in sentence A below.

5. Ⓨ Ⓝ

5. Circle the adjectives in sentence A below.

6. Ⓨ Ⓝ

Ⓐ The males have large throats.

6. Underline the verb in sentence B below.

7. Ⓨ Ⓝ

7. Circle the adverb in sentence B below.

8. Ⓨ Ⓝ

Ⓑ They also use their tails like an extra arm.

8. Circle the word below that is spelled correctly.

___ / 8
Total

chorrus

chorus

choruss

NAME: _____ DATE: _____

SCORE

Read and answer each question.

1. Ⓨ Ⓝ

1. Write the missing punctuation in the sentence.

Have you ever read stories about giant squid roaming the seas

2. Ⓨ Ⓝ

2. Write the missing punctuation in the sentence.

For ten years a group of scientists have been trying to film one.

3. Ⓨ Ⓝ

3. Circle the word that should be capitalized in the sentence.

A team from japan finally caught one on film in July 2012.

4. Ⓨ Ⓝ

4. Underline the conjunction in sentence A below.

5. Ⓨ Ⓝ

5. Circle the article in sentence A below.

6. Ⓨ Ⓝ

A It was missing two tentacles, so the squid was just ten feet long.

7. Ⓨ Ⓝ

6. Underline the adjectives in sentence B below.

7. Circle the complete subject in sentence B below.

8. Ⓨ Ⓝ

B The longest squid ever caught measured 59 feet.

___ / 8
Total

8. Circle the word below that is spelled correctly.

creture

creeture

creature

 #51170—180 Days of Language

NAME: _____ DATE: _____

DIRECTIONS Read and answer each question.

1. Write the missing punctuation in the sentence.

Gertrude Ederle didnt learn to swim until she was nine years old.

1. Ⓨ Ⓝ

2. Write the missing punctuation in the sentence.

But she became famous for her swimming on August 6 1926.

2. Ⓨ Ⓝ

3. Ⓨ Ⓝ

3. Circle the word that should be capitalized in the sentence.

She was the first woman to swim the English channel.

4. Ⓨ Ⓝ

4. Underline the prepositional phrase in sentence A below.

5. Ⓨ Ⓝ

5. Circle the possessive pronoun in sentence A below.

6. Ⓨ Ⓝ

A Her hearing was damaged during the swim.

6. Underline the preposition in sentence B below.

7. Ⓨ Ⓝ

7. Circle the proper noun in sentence B below.

8. Ⓨ Ⓝ

B Ederle became a swimming teacher for deaf children.

8. Circle the word below that is spelled correctly.

___ / 8
Total

mission

missoin

mision

NAME: _____ **DATE:** _____

SCORE

1. Ⓨ Ⓝ

2. Ⓨ Ⓝ

3. Ⓨ Ⓝ

4. Ⓨ Ⓝ

5. Ⓨ Ⓝ

6. Ⓨ Ⓝ

7. Ⓨ Ⓝ

8. Ⓨ Ⓝ

___ / 8
Total

DIRECTIONS Read and answer each question.

1. Write the missing punctuation in the sentence.

During the 1700s dating in America was very different from how it is now.

2. Write the missing punctuation in the sentence.

People worked long hours so courting waited until evening.

3. Circle the word that should be capitalized in the sentence.

People in the american colonies also lived far apart, and houses were small.

4. Underline the helping verb in sentence A below.

5. Circle the plural nouns in sentence A below.

A The parents would set up thier sons and daughters with appropriate suitors.

6. Underline the verb in sentence B below.

7. Circle the complete subject in sentence B below.

B Dates included picnics, dinners, or dancing.

8. Circle the word below that is spelled correctly.

discouregement   discuragement   discouragement

NAME: _____ **DATE:** _____

DIRECTIONS Read and answer each question.

1. Write the missing punctuation in the sentence.

Are you creative hardworking, clever, and adaptable?

1. Ⓨ Ⓝ

2. Write the missing punctuation in the sentence.

If you like taking risks you might be a good entrepreneur.

2. Ⓨ Ⓝ

3. Ⓨ Ⓝ

3. Circle the word that should be capitalized in the sentence.

Bill Gates, the founder of Microsoft corporation®, is an entrepreneur.

4. Ⓨ Ⓝ

4. Underline the pronoun in sentence A below.

5. Ⓨ Ⓝ

5. Circle the contraction in sentence A below.

Ⓐ You don't have to be an adult to be an entrepreneur.

6. Ⓨ Ⓝ

6. Underline the conjunction in sentence B below.

7. Ⓨ Ⓝ

7. Circle the adjectives in sentence B below.

Ⓑ But you do need a good idea and then to work hard!

8. Ⓨ Ⓝ

8. Circle the word below that is spelled correctly.

brilliant

brillient

briliant

____ / 8
Total

NAME: _____ DATE: _____

SCORE

1. Ⓨ Ⓝ

2. Ⓨ Ⓝ

3. Ⓨ Ⓝ

4. Ⓨ Ⓝ

5. Ⓨ Ⓝ

6. Ⓨ Ⓝ

7. Ⓨ Ⓝ

8. Ⓨ Ⓝ

___ / 8
Total

DIRECTIONS Read and answer each question.

1. Write the missing punctuation in the sentence.

If a hummingbird follows you look closely.

2. Write the missing punctuation in the sentence.

It could be a hummingbird or it could be a very small spy plane!

3. Circle the word that should be capitalized in the sentence.

there is a tiny robot hummingbird with a camera onboard.

4. Underline the preposition in sentence A below.

5. Circle the prepositional phrase in sentence A below.

Ⓐ It can be guided by a pilot.

6. Underline the helping verbs in sentence B below.

7. Circle the pronoun in sentence B below.

Ⓑ It may be used by the military or for search and rescue.

8. Circle the word below that is spelled correctly.

obeidient

obedient

obediant

NAME: _____ **DATE:** _____

DIRECTIONS Read and answer each question.

1. Write the missing punctuation in the sentence.

Every day is Valentines Day for owl monkeys.

2. Write the missing punctuation in the sentence.

Once they get together a male and female stay together.

3. Circle the word that should be capitalized in the sentence.

Found in Central America and south America, they have another special habit.

4. Underline the adverb in sentence A below.

5. Circle the article in sentence A below.

A The males are very involved dads.

6. Underline the preposition in sentence B below.

7. Circle the verbs in sentence B below.

B Males feed, carry, and play with the babies.

8. Circle the word below that is spelled correctly.

faithfully

faithfuly

faithfuley

1. Ⓨ Ⓝ

2. Ⓨ Ⓝ

3. Ⓨ Ⓝ

4. Ⓨ Ⓝ

5. Ⓨ Ⓝ

6. Ⓨ Ⓝ

7. Ⓨ Ⓝ

8. Ⓨ Ⓝ

___ / 8
Total

NAME: _____ **DATE:** _____

SCORE

DIRECTIONS Read and answer each question.

1. Write the missing punctuation in the sentence.

1. Ⓨ Ⓝ

When you walk on the beach do you search for shells?

2. Ⓨ Ⓝ

2. Write the missing punctuation in the sentence.

A sand dollar is a round, gray shell and it has a star on the back.

3. Ⓨ Ⓝ

3. Circle the word that should be capitalized in the sentence.

4. Ⓨ Ⓝ

Sand dollars are called *pansy shells* in south Africa.

5. Ⓨ Ⓝ

4. Underline the adverb in sentence A below.

5. Circle the article in sentence A below.

6. Ⓨ Ⓝ

Ⓐ A sand dollar was once alive.

7. Ⓨ Ⓝ

6. Underline the complete predicate in sentence B below.

7. Circle the possessive pronoun in sentence B below.

8. Ⓨ Ⓝ

Ⓑ It used its spines to dig in the sand.

___ / 8
Total

8. Circle the word below that is spelled correctly.

peculliar

peculier

peculiar

NAME: _____ **DATE:** _____

DIRECTIONS Read and answer each question.

SCORE

1. Write the missing punctuation in the sentence.

Have you ever watched a snake flick out its tongue

1. Ⓨ Ⓝ

2. Write the missing punctuation in the sentence.

That long forked tongue is used for smelling.

2. Ⓨ Ⓝ

3. Ⓨ Ⓝ

3. Circle the word that should be capitalized in the sentence.

Most snakes in the united States aren't poisonous.

4. Ⓨ Ⓝ

4. Underline the verb in sentence A below.

5. Ⓨ Ⓝ

5. Circle the plural nouns in sentence A below.

Ⓐ Most poisonous snakes have triangle-shaped heads.

6. Ⓨ Ⓝ

6. Underline the adverb that means "also" in sentence B below.

7. Ⓨ Ⓝ

7. Circle the adjective in sentence B below.

Ⓑ They often have slitted eyes, too.

8. Ⓨ Ⓝ

8. Circle the word below that is spelled correctly.

viscious

viceous

vicious

___ / 8
Total

NAME: _____ DATE: _____

SCORE

1. Ⓨ Ⓝ

2. Ⓨ Ⓝ

3. Ⓨ Ⓝ

4. Ⓨ Ⓝ

5. Ⓨ Ⓝ

6. Ⓨ Ⓝ

7. Ⓨ Ⓝ

8. Ⓨ Ⓝ

___ / 8
Total

DIRECTIONS   Read and answer each question.

1. Write the missing punctuation in the sentence.

Its a myth that cats always land on their feet.

2. Write the missing punctuation in the sentence.

However they usually do, and they learn how as kittens.

3. Circle the word that should be capitalized in the sentence.

One cat, named sugar, fell 19 stories and survived!

4. Underline the preposition in sentence A below.

5. Circle the prepositional phrase in sentence A below.

Ⓐ   Cats spread out their legs during a fall.

6. Underline the pronoun in sentence B below.

7. Circle the article in sentence B below.

Ⓑ   That movement spreads out the force when they hit.

8. Circle the word below that is spelled correctly.

ajjust

adjust

ajust

NAME: _____ **DATE:** _____

DIRECTIONS Read and answer each question.

1. Write the missing punctuation in the sentence.

Vampire bats feed on cows pigs, and horses.

2. Write the missing punctuation in the sentence.

Theyll fly out each night in search of something to bite.

3. Circle the word that should be capitalized in the sentence.

They can be found in mexico and other countries.

4. Underline the conjunction in sentence A below.

5. Circle the verbs in sentence A below.

A This bat bites a sleeping animal and laps up the blood.

6. Underline the contraction in sentence B below.

7. Circle the adjectives in sentence B below.

B The tiny bite doesn't even wake the animal!

8. Circle the word below that is spelled correctly.

discomfort

discoumfort

discomfurt

SCORE

1. Ⓨ Ⓝ

2. Ⓨ Ⓝ

3. Ⓨ Ⓝ

4. Ⓨ Ⓝ

5. Ⓨ Ⓝ

6. Ⓨ Ⓝ

7. Ⓨ Ⓝ

8. Ⓨ Ⓝ

___ / 8
Total

NAME: _____ DATE: _____

DIRECTIONS Read and answer each question.

SCORE

1. Ⓨ Ⓝ

1. Write the missing punctuation in the sentence.

The bald eagle isnt really bald.

2. Ⓨ Ⓝ

2. Write the missing punctuation in the sentence.

The eagles head is covered with white feathers.

3. Ⓨ Ⓝ

3. Circle the word that should be capitalized in the sentence.

4. Ⓨ Ⓝ

The bald eagle can be found throughout north America.

5. Ⓨ Ⓝ

4. Underline the verb in sentence A below.

5. Circle the preposition in sentence A below.

6. Ⓨ Ⓝ

Ⓐ The name comes from an old English word, *piebald*.

7. Ⓨ Ⓝ

6. Underline the verb in sentence B below.

7. Circle the complete subject in sentence B below.

8. Ⓨ Ⓝ

Ⓑ Piebald means "white" not "hairless."

___ / 8
Total

8. Circle the word below that is spelled correctly.

simbol

symbol

symbul

#51170—180 Days of Language   © Shell Education

NAME: _____ DATE: _____

DIRECTIONS Read and answer each question.

1. Write the missing punctuation in the sentence.

In 1947 computers were rare and complicated to use.

1. Ⓨ Ⓝ

2. Write the missing punctuation in the sentence.

Is your computer ever affected by a virus or a "bug in the software?

2. Ⓨ Ⓝ

3. Ⓨ Ⓝ

3. Circle the word that should be capitalized in the sentence.

Computers at Harvard university began having problems.

4. Ⓨ Ⓝ

4. Underline the helping verb in sentence A below.

5. Ⓨ Ⓝ

5. Circle the complete subject in sentence A below.

Ⓐ A moth was found to be caught in the computer.

6. Ⓨ Ⓝ

6. Underline the adverb in sentence B below.

7. Ⓨ Ⓝ

7. Circle the adjectives in sentence B below.

Ⓑ The computer operators carefully "debugged" the computer.

8. Ⓨ Ⓝ

8. Circle the word below that is spelled correctly.

innvestigation

investtigation

investigation

___ / 8
Total

NAME: _____ **DATE:** _____

SCORE

DIRECTIONS   Read and answer each question.

1. Ⓨ Ⓝ

1. Write the missing punctuation in the sentence.

According to legend potato chips were invented by accident.

2. Ⓨ Ⓝ

2. Write the missing punctuation in the sentence.

A customer sent back his french fries and he said they were too soggy.

3. Ⓨ Ⓝ

3. Circle the word that should be capitalized in the sentence.

4. Ⓨ Ⓝ

Annoyed, the head chef at Moon's Lake house Resort made thin, crisp chips.

5. Ⓨ Ⓝ

4. Underline the complete subject in sentence A below.

5. Circle the verb in sentence A below.

6. Ⓨ Ⓝ

Ⓐ   The customer loved them!

7. Ⓨ Ⓝ

6. Underline the complete subject in sentence B below.

7. Circle the verb in sentence B below.

8. Ⓨ Ⓝ

Ⓑ   George Crum and his sister Katie claimed to be the inventors.

___ / 8
Total

8. Circle the word below that is spelled correctly.

preference

perferrence

preferrence

NAME: _____ **DATE:** _____

DIRECTIONS Read and answer each question.

1. Write the missing punctuation in the sentence.

"*Who, who, who,* say many owls at night.

1. Ⓨ Ⓝ

2. Write the missing punctuation in the sentence.

Not all owls hoot but they all hunt.

2. Ⓨ Ⓝ

3. Ⓨ Ⓝ

3. Circle the word that should be capitalized in the sentence.

Owls are found almost everywhere except antarctica.

4. Ⓨ Ⓝ

4. Underline the compound verb in sentence A below.

5. Ⓨ Ⓝ

5. Circle the adverb in sentence A below.

Ⓐ Owls can see and hear well.

6. Ⓨ Ⓝ

6. Underline the linking verb in sentence B below.

7. Ⓨ Ⓝ

7. Circle the possessive pronoun in sentence B below.

Ⓑ Their powerful legs and sharp claws are perfect for hunting.

8. Ⓨ Ⓝ

8. Circle the word below that is spelled correctly.

midnight

midnihgt

midnite

___ / 8
Total

NAME: _____ DATE: _____

1. Ⓨ Ⓝ

2. Ⓨ Ⓝ

3. Ⓨ Ⓝ

4. Ⓨ Ⓝ

5. Ⓨ Ⓝ

6. Ⓨ Ⓝ

7. Ⓨ Ⓝ

8. Ⓨ Ⓝ

___ / 8
Total

DIRECTIONS Read and answer each question.

1. Write the missing punctuation in the sentence.

Sea otters are well suited for swimming in cold icy, or freezing waters.

2. Write the missing punctuation in the sentence.

Because of their fine fur many sea otters were killed in the 1700s.

3. Circle the word that should be capitalized in the sentence.

They almost disappeared in alaska and California.

4. Underline the complete subject in sentence A below.

5. Circle the helping verb in sentence A below.

A Sea otters and seals are now protected.

6. Underline the plural noun in sentence B below.

7. Circle the articles in sentence B below.

B A group of sea otters is called a raft.

8. Circle the word below that is spelled correctly.

preventable

preventeble

preventible

NAME: _____ **DATE:** _____

DIRECTIONS Read and answer each question.

1. Write the missing punctuation in the sentence.

Have you ever seen an ostrich

1. Ⓨ Ⓝ

2. Write the missing punctuation in the sentence.

Its the world's largest bird.

2. Ⓨ Ⓝ

3. Ⓨ Ⓝ

3. Circle the word that should be capitalized in the sentence.

the ostrich also lays the largest egg.

4. Ⓨ Ⓝ

4. Underline the plural noun in sentence A below.

5. Ⓨ Ⓝ

5. Circle the pronoun in sentence A below.

Ⓐ You could put about 20 chicken eggs into one ostrich eggs.

6. Ⓨ Ⓝ

6. Underline the possessive pronoun in sentence B below.

7. Ⓨ Ⓝ

7. Circle the conjunction in sentence B below.

Ⓑ It may take a baby a day or more to peck its way out!

8. Ⓨ Ⓝ

8. Circle the word below that is spelled correctly.

tremindous

tremendous

tremendus

___ / 8
Total

NAME: _____ **DATE:** _____

DIRECTIONS Read and answer each question.

1. (Y)(N)

1. Write the missing punctuation in the sentence.

A giraffe may have a long neck but it doesn't have much of a voice.

2. (Y)(N)

2. Write the missing punctuation in the sentence.

Theyll moo like cows to their babies.

3. (Y)(N)

3. Circle the word that should be capitalized in the sentence.

4. (Y)(N)

Found in africa, they may snort or grunt a bit.

5. (Y)(N)

4. Underline the adjectives in sentence A below.

5. Circle the linking verb in sentence A below.

6. (Y)(N)

A However, that long neck is good for two things.

7. (Y)(N)

6. Underline the conjunction in sentence B below.

7. Circle the adverb in sentence B below.

8. (Y)(N)

B They can easily reach high food, and they can see predators.

___ / 8
Total

8. Circle the word below that is spelled correctly.

obivous

obviuss

obvious

NAME: _____ DATE: _____

DIRECTIONS Read and answer each question.

1. Write the missing punctuation in the sentence.

The invention of the x-ray, which occurred in 1895 changed medicine.

1. (Y) (N)

2. Write the missing punctuation in the sentence.

The invention wasnt really planned.

2. (Y) (N)

3. (Y) (N)

3. Circle the word that should be capitalized in the sentence.

Wilhelm conrad Röntgen tried taking pictures with a cathode ray projector.

4. (Y) (N)

4. Underline the verb in sentence A below.

5. (Y) (N)

5. Circle the preposition in sentence A below.

A Photographs of his wife's hands showed her bones.

6. (Y) (N)

6. Underline the complete subject in sentence B below.

7. (Y) (N)

7. Circle the verbs in sentence B below.

B Röntgen said the *X* stood for "unknown."

8. (Y) (N)

___ / 8
Total

8. Circle the word below that is spelled correctly.

acheivement

achevement

achievement

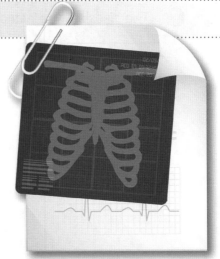

NAME: _____ **DATE:** _____

SCORE

DIRECTIONS Read and answer each question.

1. Y N

1. Write the missing punctuation in the sentence.

Just one bit of dust can make you shout, "Achoo "

2. Y N

2. Write the missing punctuation in the sentence.

Your lungs, not liking that bit of dust force it out.

3. Y N

3. Circle the word that should be capitalized in the sentence.

When you sneeze, many people say, "bless you!"

4. Y N

4. Underline the possessive pronoun in sentence A below.

5. Y N

5. Circle the preposition in sentence A below.

6. Y N

A Long ago, people thought your soul left during a sneeze.

7. Y N

6. Underline the helping verb in sentence B below.

7. Circle the preposition in sentence B below.

8. Y N

B The blessing was intended to keep you safe.

___ / 8
Total

8. Circle the word below that is spelled correctly.

religous

religious

religeous

NAME: _____ **DATE:** _____

DIRECTIONS Read and answer each question.

1. Write the missing punctuation in the sentence.

Its always fun to see butterflies in the summer.

2. Write the missing punctuation in the sentence.

After coming out of hibernation monarch butterflies look for mates.

3. Circle the word that should be capitalized in the sentence.

By March or april, they are laying their eggs.

4. Underline the complete subject in sentence A below.

5. Circle the verb in sentence A below.

A The eggs hatch into caterpillars.

6. Underline the prepositions in sentence B below.

7. Circle the helping verb in sentence B below.

B By summer, the caterpillars have changed into butterflies.

8. Circle the word below that is spelled correctly.

migrate

miggrate

migreat

1. Ⓨ Ⓝ

2. Ⓨ Ⓝ

3. Ⓨ Ⓝ

4. Ⓨ Ⓝ

5. Ⓨ Ⓝ

6. Ⓨ Ⓝ

7. Ⓨ Ⓝ

8. Ⓨ Ⓝ

___ / 8
Total

NAME: _____ DATE: _____

SCORE

DIRECTIONS Read and answer each question.

1. Ⓨ Ⓝ

1. Write the missing punctuation in the sentence.

Have you noticed that fish never blink

2. Ⓨ Ⓝ

2. Write the missing punctuation in the sentence.

Most fish cant blink because only sharks have eyelids.

3. Ⓨ Ⓝ

3. Circle the word that should be capitalized in the sentence.

4. Ⓨ Ⓝ

When asked if fish sleep, one scientist said, "most fish do rest."

5. Ⓨ Ⓝ

4. Underline the complete predicate in sentence A below.

5. Circle the complete subject in sentence A below.

6. Ⓨ Ⓝ

Ⓐ Fish do not sleep like humans do.

7. Ⓨ Ⓝ

6. Underline the contraction in sentence B below.

7. Circle the prepositional phrase in sentence B below.

8. Ⓨ Ⓝ

Ⓑ They may rest, but they're alert to danger.

___ / 8
Total

8. Circle the word below that is spelled correctly.

opponant

oponnent

opponent

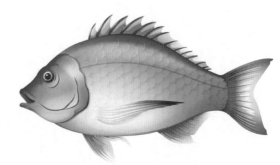

NAME: _____ **DATE:** _____

DIRECTIONS Read and answer each question.

1. Write the missing punctuation in the sentence.

Sometimes, a plane makes a sound like thunder, "Boom "

1. Ⓨ Ⓝ

2. Write the missing punctuation in the sentence.

Its called a *sonic boom.*

2. Ⓨ Ⓝ

3. Ⓨ Ⓝ

3. Circle the word that should be capitalized in the sentence.

Chuck yeager first broke the sound barrier in 1947.

4. Ⓨ Ⓝ

4. Underline the linking verb in sentence A below.

5. Ⓨ Ⓝ

5. Circle the complete predicate in sentence A below.

6. Ⓨ Ⓝ

Ⓐ That boom is a giant shock wave.

6. Underline the pronouns in sentence B below.

7. Ⓨ Ⓝ

7. Circle the noun in sentence B below.

Ⓑ It can make your house shake!

8. Ⓨ Ⓝ

8. Circle the word below that is spelled correctly.

physicle

phisycal

physical

___ / 8
Total

NAME: _____ **DATE:** _____

DIRECTIONS Read and answer each question.

1. Ⓨ Ⓝ

2. Ⓨ Ⓝ

3. Ⓨ Ⓝ

4. Ⓨ Ⓝ

5. Ⓨ Ⓝ

6. Ⓨ Ⓝ

7. Ⓨ Ⓝ

8. Ⓨ Ⓝ

___ / 8
Total

1. Write the missing punctuation in the sentence.

Drivers of cars watch for stop signs yield signs, and traffic lights.

2. Write the missing punctuation in the sentence.

In 1914, the first electric traffic lights were installed in Cleveland Ohio.

3. Circle the word that should be capitalized in the sentence.

They were placed at the corner of Euclid Avenue and east 105th Street.

4. Underline the complete subject in sentence A below.

5. Circle the prepositional phrase in sentence A below.

Ⓐ   The system had four pairs of red and green lights.

6. Underline the helping verb in sentence B below.

7. Circle the adjective that modifies *lights* in sentence B below.

Ⓑ   In 1920, traffic lights were developed with red, green, and amber.

8. Circle the word below that is spelled correctly.

vehickle

vehicle

vehiccle

NAME: _____ **DATE:** _____

DIRECTIONS Read and answer each question.

1. Write the missing punctuation in the sentence.

Perhaps its just a story, but the sandwich may have been invented by an earl.

1. (Y) (N)

2. Write the missing punctuation in the sentence.

In England being an earl showed you were important.

2. (Y) (N)

3. (Y) (N)

3. Circle the word that should be capitalized in the sentence.

John Montagu was the fourth Earl of sandwich, England.

4. (Y) (N)

4. Underline the conjunction in sentence A below.

5. (Y) (N)

5. Circle the contraction in sentence A below.

6. (Y) (N)

A One day, he was playing cards and didn't want to stop.

6. Underline the article in sentence B below.

7. (Y) (N)

7. Circle the pronoun in sentence B below.

8. (Y) (N)

B He asked for meat between slices of bread, and the rest is history!

___ / 8
Total

8. Circle the word below that is spelled correctly.

royelt

royalty

royallty

NAME: _____ DATE: _____

SCORE

DIRECTIONS Read and answer each question.

1. Ⓨ Ⓝ

1. Write the missing punctuation in the sentence.

....

Do you put grape strawberry, or raspberry jelly on your toast?

....

2. Ⓨ Ⓝ

2. Write the missing punctuation in the sentence.

....

As early as the 1600s recipes for making jam were published in America.

3. Ⓨ Ⓝ

....

3. Circle the word that should be capitalized in the sentence.

....

4. Ⓨ Ⓝ

During World war I, overseas soldiers were sent "grapelade."

....

5. Ⓨ Ⓝ

4. Underline the pronoun in sentence A below.

5. Circle the preposition in sentence A below.

6. Ⓨ Ⓝ

....

Ⓐ After the soldiers returned home, they wanted more grapelade.

....

7. Ⓨ Ⓝ

6. Underline the conjunction in sentence B below.

7. Circle the linking verb in sentence B below.

8. Ⓨ Ⓝ

....

Ⓑ Grape jelly is still a favorite of kids and adults!

....

___ / 8
Total

8. Circle the word below that is spelled correctly.

....

devoure

divour

devour

....

#51170—180 Days of Language
© Shell Education

NAME: _____ DATE: _____

DIRECTIONS Read and answer each question.

1. Write the missing punctuation in the sentence.

On August 8 1829, the first steam locomotive in America rolled down the tracks.

1. Ⓨ Ⓝ

2. Write the missing punctuation in the sentence.

Built for hauling coal, the tracks were in Honesdale Pennsylvania.

2. Ⓨ Ⓝ

3. Ⓨ Ⓝ

3. Circle the word that should be capitalized in the sentence.

The locomotive was called the Stourbridge lion.

4. Ⓨ Ⓝ

4. Underline the complete subject in sentence A below.

5. Ⓨ Ⓝ

5. Circle the prepositional phrase in sentence A below.

6. Ⓨ Ⓝ

Ⓐ The engine had a lion painted on its front.

6. Underline the common noun in sentence B below.

7. Ⓨ Ⓝ

7. Circle the proper noun in sentence B below.

8. Ⓨ Ⓝ

Ⓑ The locomotive is owned by the Smithsonian Institution.

____ / 8
Total

8. Circle the word below that is spelled correctly.

engineer

enginere

engeneer

NAME: _____ DATE: _____

DIRECTIONS Read and answer each question.

SCORE

1. Ⓨ Ⓝ

1. Write the missing punctuation in the sentence.

When a giant panda is born, it isnt exactly giant.

2. Ⓨ Ⓝ

2. Write the missing punctuation in the sentence.

Cubs, which weigh a few ounces at birth will gain about 300 pounds.

3. Ⓨ Ⓝ

3. Circle the word that should be capitalized in the sentence.

Wild pandas only live in remote areas of china.

4. Ⓨ Ⓝ

4. Underline the linking verb in sentence A below.

5. Circle the plural noun in sentence A below.

5. Ⓨ Ⓝ

6. Ⓨ Ⓝ

Ⓐ There are only about 1,000 giant pandas left in the wild.

7. Ⓨ Ⓝ

6. Underline the verb in sentence B below.

7. Circle the adjective in sentence B below.

8. Ⓨ Ⓝ

Ⓑ Scientists study captive pandas at zoos.

___ / 8
Total

8. Circle the word below that is spelled correctly.

disappear

dissappear

dissapear

NAME: _____ **DATE:** _____

DIRECTIONS Read and answer each question.

1. Write the missing punctuation in the sentence.

If you ever need help you should know about the SOS signal.

1. Ⓨ Ⓝ

2. Write the missing punctuation in the sentence.

The letters, coming from the dots and dashes of Morse code, dont stand for words.

2. Ⓨ Ⓝ

3. Ⓨ Ⓝ

3. Circle the word that should be capitalized in the sentence.

The first use of SOS was in 1908 by wireless operators on the SS *arapahoe*.

4. Ⓨ Ⓝ

4. Underline the linking verb in sentence A below.

5. Ⓨ Ⓝ

5. Circle the preposition in sentence A below.

6. Ⓨ Ⓝ

Ⓐ Before then, there were several distress signals.

6. Underline the plural noun in sentence B below.

7. Ⓨ Ⓝ

7. Circle the helping verb in sentence B below.

8. Ⓨ Ⓝ

Ⓑ Now, all countries have agreed to have one signal.

___ / 8
Total

8. Circle the word below that is spelled correctly.

establesh

esstablish

establish

NAME: _____ DATE: _____

SCORE

1. Ⓨ Ⓝ

2. Ⓨ Ⓝ

3. Ⓨ Ⓝ

4. Ⓨ Ⓝ

5. Ⓨ Ⓝ

6. Ⓨ Ⓝ

7. Ⓨ Ⓝ

8. Ⓨ Ⓝ

___ / 8
Total

DIRECTIONS Read and answer each question.

1. Write the missing punctuation in the sentence.

"Nighty-night, sleep tight. Don't let the bedbugs bite.

2. Write the missing punctuation in the sentence.

Theres a story about that rhyme.

3. Circle the word that should be capitalized in the sentence.

in colonial days, people had to tighten the ropes under beds.

4. Underline the plural noun in sentence A below.

5. Circle the adverb in sentence A below.

Ⓐ But the "sleep tight" part refers to sleeping soundly not tight ropes.

6. Underline the helping verb in sentence B below.

7. Circle the article in sentence B below.

Ⓑ As for the rest, that does refer to bedbugs!

8. Circle the word below that is spelled correctly.

hygeine

hygene

hygiene

NAME: _____ DATE: _____

DIRECTIONS Read and answer each question.

SCORE

1. Write the missing punctuation in the sentence.

When your dentist says, "Open wide, do you think about the chair you are in?

2. Write the missing punctuation in the sentence.

In the early 1800s dentists added features such as headrests to chairs.

3. Circle the word that should be capitalized in the sentence.

Mr. M. waldo Hanchett was granted the first patent for his dentist chair design.

4. Underline the adjectives in sentence A below.

5. Circle the conjunction in sentence A below.

A It had a headrest and an adjustable seat and back.

6. Underline the preposition in sentence B below.

7. Circle the helping verb in sentence B below.

B A modern dental chair can cost thousands of dollars.

8. Circle the word below that is spelled correctly.

exammination

examination

examanation

1. Ⓨ Ⓝ

2. Ⓨ Ⓝ

3. Ⓨ Ⓝ

4. Ⓨ Ⓝ

5. Ⓨ Ⓝ

6. Ⓨ Ⓝ

7. Ⓨ Ⓝ

8. Ⓨ Ⓝ

___ / 8
Total

NAME: _____ **DATE:** _____

SCORE

DIRECTIONS Read and answer each question.

1. (Y)(N)

1. Write the missing punctuation in the sentence.

Do you know how ships travel between the Atlantic and Pacific oceans

2. (Y)(N)

2. Write the missing punctuation in the sentence.

They can go around South America or they can use a shortcut.

3. (Y)(N)

3. Circle the word that should be capitalized in the sentence.

4. (Y)(N)

The shortcut is the Panama canal.

5. (Y)(N)

4. Underline the complete subject in sentence A below.

5. Circle the linking verb in sentence A below.

6. (Y)(N)

A The canal is about 48 to 51 miles (77 to 82 km) long.

7. (Y)(N)

6. Underline the article in sentence B below.

7. Circle the plural noun in sentence B below.

8. (Y)(N)

B A ship needs about eight to ten hours to get through.

_____ / 8
Total

8. Circle the word below that is spelled correctly.

detour

detoure

deetour

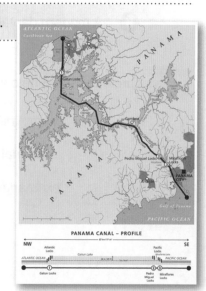

#51170—180 Days of Language

© Shell Education

NAME: _____ **DATE:** _____

DIRECTIONS Read and answer each question.

1. Write the missing punctuation in the sentence.

In the 1700s a new amusement was invited for the cold weather.

1. Ⓨ Ⓝ

2. Write the missing punctuation in the sentence.

A steep hill of ice was built and sometimes it had bumps at the end.

2. Ⓨ Ⓝ

3. Ⓨ Ⓝ

3. Circle the word that should be capitalized in the sentence.

People in russia rode down these hills in sleds made of wood or ice.

4. Ⓨ Ⓝ

4. Underline the past tense verb in sentence A below.

5. Ⓨ Ⓝ

5. Circle the articles in sentence A below.

A The ice slides inspired a ride you might go on often.

6. Ⓨ Ⓝ

6. Underline the pronoun in sentence B below.

7. Ⓨ Ⓝ

7. Circle the prepositions in sentence B below.

8. Ⓨ Ⓝ

B The next time you ride a roller coaster, think about riding on an icy sled!

___ / 8
Total

8. Circle the word below that is spelled correctly.

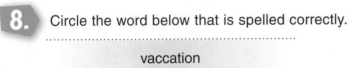

vaccation

vacation

vacattion

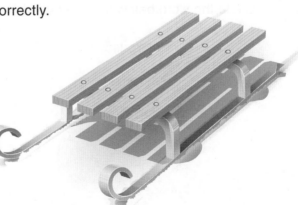

NAME: _____ **DATE:** _____

DIRECTIONS Read and answer each question.

1. (Y) (N)

1. Write the missing punctuation in the sentence.

In 1819 the first steamboat built in America crossed the ocean.

2. (Y) (N)

2. Write the missing punctuation in the sentence.

For 24 days the ship used the engine or its sails to cross.

3. (Y) (N)

3. Circle the word that should be capitalized in the sentence.

The ship was named the US *savannah* after its home port in Georgia.

4. (Y) (N)

4. Underline the preposition in sentence A below.

5. Circle the adjective in sentence A below.

5. (Y) (N)

6. (Y) (N)

A Its return trip was entirely by sail.

7. (Y) (N)

6. Underline the pronoun in sentence B below.

7. Circle the proper noun in sentence B below.

8. (Y) (N)

B It ran aground near Long Island two years later.

___ / 8
Total

8. Circle the word below that is spelled correctly.

enterprise

interprise

interprize

#51170—180 Days of Language

NAME: _____ DATE: _____

Read and answer each question.

SCORE

1. Write the missing punctuation in the sentence.

If you thought dragons lived only in stories, youd be wrong.

1. Ⓨ Ⓝ

2. Write the missing punctuation in the sentence.

Of course these dragons don't breathe fire.

2. Ⓨ Ⓝ

3. Ⓨ Ⓝ

3. Circle the word that should be capitalized in the sentence.

However, Komodo dragons, found in indonesia, are dangerous!

4. Ⓨ Ⓝ

4. Underline the pronoun in sentence A below.

5. Ⓨ Ⓝ

5. Circle the conjunction in sentence A below.

Ⓐ They are ten feet long and weigh more than 300 pounds.

6. Ⓨ Ⓝ

6. Underline the complete subject in sentence B below.

7. Ⓨ Ⓝ

7. Circle the helping verb in sentence B below.

Ⓑ Its bite can give you blood poisoning.

8. Ⓨ Ⓝ

8. Circle the word below that is spelled correctly.

miserrable

miserible

miserable

___ / 8
Total

NAME: _____ **DATE:** _____

SCORE

DIRECTIONS Read and answer each question.

1. Ⓨ Ⓝ

1. Write the missing punctuation in the sentence.

If you lived in the 1800s, youd probably have a job.

2. Ⓨ Ⓝ

2. Write the missing punctuation in the sentence.

Children worked in factories mills, and the fields.

3. Ⓨ Ⓝ

3. Circle the word that should be capitalized in the sentence.

4. Ⓨ Ⓝ

The National Child Labor committee was formed in 1904.

5. Ⓨ Ⓝ

4. Underline the complete subject in sentence A below.

5. Circle the verb in sentence A below.

6. Ⓨ Ⓝ

Ⓐ Laws were passed to keep young children from working.

7. Ⓨ Ⓝ

6. Underline the conjunction in sentence B below.

7. Circle the helping verb in sentence B below.

8. Ⓨ Ⓝ

Ⓑ Children were required to go to school until age 12 or older.

___ / 8
Total

8. Circle the word below that is spelled correctly.

education   edducation   educcation

NAME: _____ DATE: _____

DIRECTIONS Read and answer each question.

1. Write the missing punctuation in the sentence.

You may think itd be easy to be a clown.

1. Ⓨ Ⓝ

2. Write the missing punctuation in the sentence.

To be a good clown you should go to clown college.

2. Ⓨ Ⓝ

3. Ⓨ Ⓝ

3. Circle the word that should be capitalized in the sentence.

The Ringling Bros. Clown College is in venice, Florida.

4. Ⓨ Ⓝ

4. Underline the complete predicate in sentence A below.

5. Ⓨ Ⓝ

5. Circle the pronoun in sentence A below.

6. Ⓨ Ⓝ

A You need to try out to get into clown college.

6. Underline the contraction in sentence B below.

7. Ⓨ Ⓝ

7. Circle the conjunction in sentence B below.

8. Ⓨ Ⓝ

B If you are accepted, that's when the fun and work begin!

8. Circle the word below that is spelled correctly.

___ / 8
Total

audience

audiense

auddience

NAME: _____ **DATE:** _____

SCORE

DIRECTIONS Read and answer each question.

1. (Y)(N)

1. Write the missing punctuation in the sentence.

Have you ever run in a marathon

2. (Y)(N)

2. Write the missing punctuation in the sentence.

According to legend the word *marathon* honors a soldier.

3. (Y)(N)

3. Circle the word that should be capitalized in the sentence.

4. (Y)(N)

Pheidippides, a Greek soldier, ran from Marathon to athens without stopping.

5. (Y)(N)

4. Underline the proper noun in sentence A below.

5. Circle the pronoun in sentence A below.

6. (Y)(N)

A He announced that the Greeks had won a battle.

7. (Y)(N)

6. Underline the conjunction in sentence B below.

7. Circle the adjectives in sentence B below.

8. (Y)(N)

B Then, the exhausted soldier fell down and died.

____ / 8
Total

8. Circle the word below that is spelled correctly.

tournement

tournament

tournameant

#51170—180 Days of Language

© Shell Education

NAME: _____ DATE: _____

SCORE

DIRECTIONS Read and answer each question.

1. Write the missing punctuation in the sentence.

After 73 years underwater the wrecked *Titanic* was found.

1. Ⓨ Ⓝ

2. Write the missing punctuation in the sentence.

Dr Robert Ballard led the team that found the ship.

2. Ⓨ Ⓝ

3. Ⓨ Ⓝ

3. Circle the word that should be capitalized in the sentence.

A team of American and french researchers had searched together.

4. Ⓨ Ⓝ

4. Underline the possessive pronoun in sentence A below.

5. Ⓨ Ⓝ

5. Circle the verb in sentence A below.

Ⓐ The team used undersea robots in their search.

6. Ⓨ Ⓝ

6. Underline the complete subject in sentence B below.

7. Ⓨ Ⓝ

7. Circle the verb in sentence B below.

Ⓑ The ship sank on its first voyage after hitting an iceberg.

8. Ⓨ Ⓝ

8. Circle the word below that is spelled correctly.

disastter

dissaster

disaster

___ / 8
Total

NAME: _____ DATE: _____

1. Ⓨ Ⓝ

2. Ⓨ Ⓝ

3. Ⓨ Ⓝ

4. Ⓨ Ⓝ

5. Ⓨ Ⓝ

6. Ⓨ Ⓝ

7. Ⓨ Ⓝ

8. Ⓨ Ⓝ

___ / 8
Total

DIRECTIONS Read and answer each question.

1. Write the missing punctuation in the sentence.

In 1905, a boy left water powdered soda, and a stick in a cup outside.

2. Write the missing punctuation in the sentence.

It was a cold night and the mixture froze.

3. Circle the word that should be capitalized in the sentence.

Frank epperson found it the next morning and called it the *Epsicle.*

4. Underline the preposition in sentence A below.

5. Circle the possessive noun in sentence A below.

Ⓐ   When Frank had kids, they begged for Pop's 'sicle.

6. Underline the pronouns in sentence B below.

7. Circle the proper noun in sentence B below.

Ⓑ   In 1923, he changed the name to a treat you know—the Popsicle®!

8. Circle the word below that is spelled correctly.

compliment

complimment

complimint

NAME: _____ **DATE:** _____

DIRECTIONS Read and answer each question.

SCORE

1. Write the missing punctuation in the sentence.

"Write what you know about, many writing teachers say.

1. Ⓨ Ⓝ

2. Write the missing punctuation in the sentence.

Roald Dahl, author of many books often did just that.

2. Ⓨ Ⓝ

3. Ⓨ Ⓝ

3. Circle the word that should be capitalized in the sentence.

While in school, the students sometimes got cadbury chocolate bars to test.

4. Ⓨ Ⓝ

4. Underline the complete subject in sentence A below.

5. Ⓨ Ⓝ

5. Circle the verb in sentence A below.

6. Ⓨ Ⓝ

Ⓐ   Dahl dreamed of working in a chocolate company.

7. Ⓨ Ⓝ

6. Circle the book title in sentence B below.

7. Underline the possessive pronoun in sentence B below.

8. Ⓨ Ⓝ

Ⓑ   Those chocolate bars inspired his writing of <u>Charlie and the Chocolate Factory</u>.

___ / 8
Total

8. Circle the word below that is spelled correctly.

subjeck

subbject

subject

NAME: _____   **DATE:** _____

SCORE

DIRECTIONS   Read and answer each question.

1. Ⓨ Ⓝ

1. Write the missing punctuation in the sentence.

If you want to hold two pieces of paper together you might use a stapler.

2. Ⓨ Ⓝ

2. Write the missing punctuation in the sentence.

In 1841 the first patent for a stapler was issued.

3. Ⓨ Ⓝ

3. Circle the word that should be capitalized in the sentence.

Samuel slocum, the inventor, didn't call it a stapler.

4. Ⓨ Ⓝ

4. Underline the verb in sentence A below.

5. Ⓨ Ⓝ

5. Circle the pronouns in sentence A below.

6. Ⓨ Ⓝ

Ⓐ   He called it a "machine for sticking pins into paper."

7. Ⓨ Ⓝ

6. Underline the possessive pronoun in sentence B below.

7. Circle the noun in sentence B below.

8. Ⓨ Ⓝ

Ⓑ   What would you name his invention?

___ / 8
Total

8. Circle the word below that is spelled correctly.

suggestion

suggesttion

sugestion

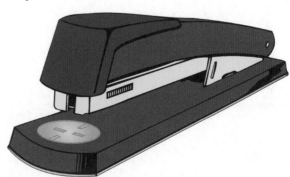

#51170—180 Days of Language

NAME: _____ **DATE:** _____

DIRECTIONS Read and answer each question.

SCORE

1. Write the missing punctuation in the sentence.

If you grew up in the 50s you probably shopped at a dime store.

1. Ⓨ Ⓝ

2. Write the missing punctuation in the sentence.

Many of the items in the store cost a nickel a dime, or a quarter.

2. Ⓨ Ⓝ

3. Ⓨ Ⓝ

3. Circle the word that should be capitalized in the sentence.

Two popular five-and-dime stores were Woolworth's and Ben franklin.

4. Ⓨ Ⓝ

4. Underline the preposition in sentence A below.

5. Ⓨ Ⓝ

5. Circle the prepositional phrase in sentence A below.

Ⓐ Children loved shopping for candy and toys.

6. Ⓨ Ⓝ

6. Underline the complete predicate in sentence B below.

7. Ⓨ Ⓝ

7. Circle the verb in sentence B below.

Ⓑ People today shop for bargains at dollar stores.

8. Ⓨ Ⓝ

8. Circle the word below that is spelled correctly.

various

variouss

varrious

___ / 8
Total

NAME: _____ DATE: _____

DIRECTIONS Read and answer each question.

1. Ⓨ Ⓝ

2. Ⓨ Ⓝ

3. Ⓨ Ⓝ

4. Ⓨ Ⓝ

5. Ⓨ Ⓝ

6. Ⓨ Ⓝ

7. Ⓨ Ⓝ

8. Ⓨ Ⓝ

___ / 8
Total

1. Write the missing punctuation in the sentence.

Bette Greene, who became a successful writer got just average grades.

2. Write the missing punctuation in the sentence.

That didnt stop her from thinking she was a great writer.

3. Circle the word that should be capitalized in the sentence.

One book, <u>Summer of My German soldier</u>, was turned down 17 times by publishers.

4. Underline the conjunction in sentence A below.

5. Circle the possessive pronoun in sentence A below.

Ⓐ She writes her books in ink and rewrites on the computer.

6. Underline the complete subject in sentence B below.

7. Circle the prepositional phrase in sentence B below.

Ⓑ She likes the drama of writing in ink.

8. Circle the word below that is spelled correctly.

chalenge   challege   challenge

NAME: _____ **DATE:** _____

DIRECTIONS Read and answer each question.

1. Write the missing punctuation in the sentence.

For 25 long minutes Nik Wallenda walked on a tightrope.

2. Write the missing punctuation in the sentence.

Its his job to walk on a tightrope, but this was special.

3. Circle the word that should be capitalized in the sentence.

This walk was 200 feet (60 m) above Niagara falls.

4. Underline the preposition in sentence A below.

5. Circle the adjective in sentence A below.

A Crowds watched as he crossed in heavy winds.

6. Underline the complete subject in sentence B below.

7. Circle the verb in sentence B below.

B His grandfather died in a high-wire act at age 73.

8. Circle the word below that is spelled correctly.

conqure

conquer

conquerr

1. Ⓨ Ⓝ

2. Ⓨ Ⓝ

3. Ⓨ Ⓝ

4. Ⓨ Ⓝ

5. Ⓨ Ⓝ

6. Ⓨ Ⓝ

7. Ⓨ Ⓝ

8. Ⓨ Ⓝ

___ / 8
Total

NAME: _____ DATE: _____

SCORE

DIRECTIONS Read and answer each question.

1. (Y)(N)

1. Write the missing punctuation in the sentence.

"Everybody in my family paints—excluding possibly the dogs, said James Wyeth.

2. (Y)(N)

2. Write the missing punctuation in the sentence.

Born in 1946 he left school in sixth grade so he could paint more.

3. (Y)(N)

3. Circle the word that should be capitalized in the sentence.

4. (Y)(N)

He studied with his Aunt carolyn and also got advice from his father.

5. (Y)(N)

4. Underline the helping verb in sentence A below.

5. Circle the adjectives in sentence A below.

6. (Y)(N)

A He has painted portraits of many famous politicians.

7. (Y)(N)

6. Underline the verb in sentence B below.

7. Circle the possessive pronoun in sentence B below.

8. (Y)(N)

B His work hangs in museums around the world.

___ / 8
Total

8. Circle the word below that is spelled correctly.

compossition

composition

compposition

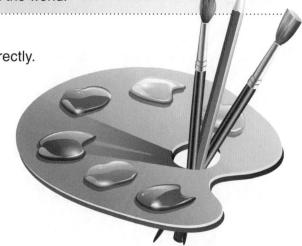

NAME: _____ DATE: _____

DIRECTIONS Read and answer each question.

1. Write the missing punctuation in the sentence.

"Slow and steady wins the race is good advice.

1. Ⓨ Ⓝ

2. Write the missing punctuation in the sentence.

For hundreds of years people have been reading fables.

2. Ⓨ Ⓝ

3. Ⓨ Ⓝ

3. Circle the word that should be capitalized in the sentence.

Jean de la Fontaine was born in france.

4. Ⓨ Ⓝ

4. Underline the complete subject in sentence A below.

5. Circle the verb in sentence A below.

5. Ⓨ Ⓝ

A Fontaine wrote more than 200 fables.

6. Ⓨ Ⓝ

6. Underline the adjectives in sentence B below.

7. Ⓨ Ⓝ

7. Circle the preposition in sentence B below.

B Fables are small stories with big lessons.

8. Ⓨ Ⓝ

8. Circle the word below that is spelled correctly.

seriuos

serrious

serious

___ / 8
Total

NAME: _____   DATE: _____

Read and answer each question.

SCORE

1. Ⓨ Ⓝ

1. Write the missing punctuation in the sentence.

Do you have a soda candy, or popcorn at the movies?

2. Ⓨ Ⓝ

2. Write the missing punctuation in the sentence.

Popcorn, which has been around for a long time can be a tasty snack.

3. Ⓨ Ⓝ

3. Circle the word that should be capitalized in the sentence.

Popcorn was used in Aztec indian ceremonies in the 1500s.

4. Ⓨ Ⓝ

4. Underline the complete subject in sentence A below.

5. Ⓨ Ⓝ

5. Circle the article in sentence A below.

6. Ⓨ Ⓝ

Ⓐ Explorers wrote about corn that burst into a flower when toasted.

7. Ⓨ Ⓝ

6. Underline the verb in sentence B below.

7. Circle the complete subject in sentence B below.

8. Ⓨ Ⓝ

Ⓑ Colonists ate popcorn with cream and sugar for breakfast.

___ / 8
Total

8. Circle the word below that is spelled correctly.

favorite

favorrite

faverite

  #51170—180 Days of Language

NAME: _____ **DATE:** _____

DIRECTIONS Read and answer each question.

1. Write the missing punctuation in the sentence.

On April 2, 1805 a great storyteller was born.

1. Ⓨ Ⓝ

2. Write the missing punctuation in the sentence.

His father was a shoemaker and his mother washed clothes to earn money.

2. Ⓨ Ⓝ

3. Ⓨ Ⓝ

3. Circle the word that should be capitalized in the sentence.

Hans christian Andersen wasn't a great student, but he liked to write.

4. Ⓨ Ⓝ

4. Underline the pronoun in sentence A below.

5. Ⓨ Ⓝ

5. Circle the conjunction in sentence A below.

A He retold folktales and made up new stories.

6. Ⓨ Ⓝ

6. Underline the adjectives in sentence B below.

7. Ⓨ Ⓝ

7. Circle the proper noun in sentence B below.

B Andersen has been called the father of the modern fairy tale.

8. Ⓨ Ⓝ

8. Circle the word below that is spelled correctly.

___ / 8
Total

marvellous   marvelous   marveluos

NAME: _____   DATE: _____

DIRECTIONS   Read and answer each question.

SCORE

1. Ⓨ Ⓝ

1. Write the missing punctuation in the sentence.

After decades of being called a planet Pluto lost that label.

2. Ⓨ Ⓝ

2. Write the missing punctuation in the sentence.

Its now called a *dwarf planet*.

3. Ⓨ Ⓝ

3. Circle the word that should be capitalized in the sentence.

Pluto was discovered in 1930 at the Lowell observatory in Arizona.

4. Ⓨ Ⓝ

4. Underline the possessive pronoun in sentence A below.

5. Circle the helping verb in sentence A below.

5. Ⓨ Ⓝ

6. Ⓨ Ⓝ

Ⓐ   Its name was suggested by a girl in England.

7. Ⓨ Ⓝ

6. Underline the preposition in sentence B below.

7. Circle the adjectives in sentence B below.

8. Ⓨ Ⓝ

Ⓑ   Pluto is the name of a mythological god.

___ / 8
Total

8. Circle the word below that is spelled correctly.

suitable

suiteble

suittable

NAME: _____ DATE: _____

DIRECTIONS Read and answer each question.

1. Write the missing punctuation in the sentence.

Venice, a city in Italy is built on more than 100 islands.

2. Write the missing punctuation in the sentence.

To get around, you can ride in gondolas water taxis, or water-buses.

3. Circle the word that should be capitalized in the sentence.

Don't miss the Grand canal if you visit.

4. Underline the adjectives in sentence A below.

5. Circle the prepositional phrase in sentence A below.

A It resembles a winding snake from the sky.

6. Underline the linking verb in sentence B below.

7. Circle the proper noun in sentence B below.

B Venice is famous for its canals, art, and beautiful buildings.

8. Circle the word below that is spelled correctly.

picture

pichure

pitchure

1. Ⓨ Ⓝ

2. Ⓨ Ⓝ

3. Ⓨ Ⓝ

4. Ⓨ Ⓝ

5. Ⓨ Ⓝ

6. Ⓨ Ⓝ

7. Ⓨ Ⓝ

8. Ⓨ Ⓝ

___ / 8
Total

© Shell Education

#51170—180 Days of Language

NAME: _____ DATE: _____

DIRECTIONS Read and answer each question.

SCORE

1. Ⓨ Ⓝ

1. Write the missing punctuation in the sentence.

This salamander has many names but the funniest is snot otter.

2. Ⓨ Ⓝ

2. Write the missing punctuation in the sentence.

It has a large, flat body and it has thick folds on its sides.

3. Ⓨ Ⓝ

3. Circle the word that should be capitalized in the sentence.

They can be found in the eastern United states.

4. Ⓨ Ⓝ

4. Underline the complete subject in sentence A below.

5. Ⓨ Ⓝ

5. Circle the adjective in sentence A below.

Ⓐ Snot otters live in shallow streams.

6. Ⓨ Ⓝ

6. Underline the verb in sentence B below.

7. Ⓨ Ⓝ

7. Circle the conjunction in sentence B below.

Ⓑ They eat crayfish and small fish.

8. Ⓨ Ⓝ

____ / 8
Total

8. Circle the word below that is spelled correctly.

obsserve

obsearve

observe

NAME: _____ DATE: _____

DIRECTIONS Read and answer each question.

1. Write the missing punctuation in the sentence.

If you like haunted houses you should tour the Myrtles Plantation.

1. Ⓨ Ⓝ

2. Write the missing punctuation in the sentence.

Built in 1796 in St. Francisville Louisiana, it is said to have several ghosts.

2. Ⓨ Ⓝ

3. Ⓨ Ⓝ

3. Circle the word that should be capitalized in the sentence.

The most famous ghost is chloe, a former slave, who even shows up in pictures.

4. Ⓨ Ⓝ

4. Underline the verbs in sentence A below.

5. Ⓨ Ⓝ

5. Circle the complete subject in sentence A below.

A Other ghost slaves appear and ask if there are chores to do.

6. Ⓨ Ⓝ

6. Underline the complete predicate in sentence B below.

7. Ⓨ Ⓝ

7. Circle the verb in sentence B below.

B The piano plays by itself sometimes!

8. Ⓨ Ⓝ

8. Circle the word below that is spelled correctly.

presence

pressence

precense

___ / 8
Total

NAME: _____ **DATE:** _____

1. (Y)(N)

2. (Y)(N)

3. (Y)(N)

4. (Y)(N)

5. (Y)(N)

6. (Y)(N)

7. (Y)(N)

8. (Y)(N)

___ / 8
Total

DIRECTIONS Read and answer each question.

1. Write the missing punctuation in the sentence.

The first U.S. president, George Washington owned ten hound dogs.

2. Write the missing punctuation in the sentence.

Some of their names were Mopsey, Tipier Sweetlips, and Searcher.

3. Circle the word that should be capitalized in the sentence.

President Franklin D. roosevelt had a sense of humor when it came to dog names.

4. Underline the pronouns in sentence A below.

5. Circle the verb in sentence A below.

A He named his English sheepdog Tiny.

6. Underline the helping verb in sentence B below.

7. Circle the possessive pronoun in sentence B below.

B His Great Dane was named President!

8. Circle the word below that is spelled correctly.

choise

choice

choicse

NAME: _____ DATE: _____

DIRECTIONS Read and answer each question.

1. Write the missing punctuation in the sentence.

Since 1922 3-D movies have been produced.

1. Ⓨ Ⓝ

2. Write the missing punctuation in the sentence.

However it took about 40 years for 3-D movies to get popular.

2. Ⓨ Ⓝ

3. Ⓨ Ⓝ

3. Circle the word that should be capitalized in the sentence.

The Walt Disney company began making 3-D movies in 1985.

4. Ⓨ Ⓝ

4. Underline the complete subject in sentence A below.

5. Ⓨ Ⓝ

5. Circle the helping verb in sentence A below.

A Some movies are produced in both 2-D and 3-D.

6. Ⓨ Ⓝ

6. Underline the article in sentence B below.

7. Ⓨ Ⓝ

7. Circle the plural noun in sentence B below.

B Moviegoers who prefer 2-D appreciate having a choice.

8. Ⓨ Ⓝ

8. Circle the word below that is spelled correctly.

greatful

gratefull

grateful

___ / 8
Total

NAME: _____ **DATE:** _____

SCORE

1. (Y)(N)

2. (Y)(N)

3. (Y)(N)

4. (Y)(N)

5. (Y)(N)

6. (Y)(N)

7. (Y)(N)

8. (Y)(N)

___ / 8
Total

DIRECTIONS Read and answer each question.

1. Write the missing punctuation in the sentence.

Do you know how the Liberty Bell got its crack

2. Write the missing punctuation in the sentence.

The bell, made of a mix of metals cracked when tested.

3. Circle the word that should be capitalized in the sentence.

It was recast twice, and the makers in london thought it was fine.

4. Underline the preposition in sentence A below.

5. Circle the prepositional phrase in sentence A below.

A It may have cracked during the Revolutionary War.

6. Underline the proper noun in sentence B below.

7. Circle the adjectives in sentence B below.

B You can see the famous bell in Philadelphia.

8. Circle the word below that is spelled correctly.

mysterious

myssterious

mysterrious

NAME: _____ DATE: _____

DIRECTIONS Read and answer each question.

1. Write the missing punctuation in the sentence.

"Eat your carrots. They're good for your eyes " your mother may say.

1. Ⓨ Ⓝ

2. Write the missing punctuation in the sentence.

Theres a story that may have helped spread that idea.

2. Ⓨ Ⓝ

3. Ⓨ Ⓝ

3. Circle the word that should be capitalized in the sentence.

A british fighter pilot during World War II said carrots helped his night vision.

4. Ⓨ Ⓝ

4. Underline the helping verb in sentence A below.

5. Ⓨ Ⓝ

5. Circle the preposition in sentence A below.

A But the British really were using radar at night.

6. Ⓨ Ⓝ

6. Underline the conjunction in sentence B below.

7. Ⓨ Ⓝ

7. Circle the complete subject in sentence B below.

B People believed the story and grew lots of carrots!

8. Ⓨ Ⓝ

8. Circle the word below that is spelled correctly.

twillight

twilite

twilight

____ / 8
Total

NAME: _____ DATE: _____

DIRECTIONS Read and answer each question.

SCORE

1. Ⓨ Ⓝ

2. Ⓨ Ⓝ

3. Ⓨ Ⓝ

4. Ⓨ Ⓝ

5. Ⓨ Ⓝ

6. Ⓨ Ⓝ

7. Ⓨ Ⓝ

8. Ⓨ Ⓝ

___ / 8
Total

1. Write the missing punctuation in the sentence.

If you sneeze when you go outside, youre not alone.

2. Write the missing punctuation in the sentence.

Scientists arent sure why one in three people do this.

3. Circle the word that should be capitalized in the sentence.

Even aristotle, who lived more than 2,000 years ago, wondered why.

4. Underline the conjunction in sentence A below.

5. Circle the possessive pronoun in sentence A below.

Ⓐ Perhaps you need to blink, so your brain tricks you with a sneeze.

6. Underline the pronoun in sentence B below.

7. Circle the plural noun in sentence B below.

Ⓑ Scientists do know that you can't stop that sneeze!

8. Circle the word below that is spelled correctly.

stubburn

stuborn

stubborn

NAME: _____ DATE: _____

DIRECTIONS Read and answer each question.

1. Write the missing punctuation in the sentence.

Wouldnt you like to be treated like a queen?

1. Ⓨ Ⓝ

2. Write the missing punctuation in the sentence.

If you were a naked mole rat perhaps you'd be the queen.

2. Ⓨ Ⓝ

3. Ⓨ Ⓝ

3. Circle the word that should be capitalized in the sentence.

You can see these cute rodents at the Pacific Science center in Seattle.

4. Ⓨ Ⓝ

4. Underline the complete subject in sentence A below.

5. Ⓨ Ⓝ

5. Circle the adjective in sentence A below.

Ⓐ Worker rats dig burrows or gather food.

6. Ⓨ Ⓝ

6. Underline the adjectives in sentence B below.

7. Ⓨ Ⓝ

7. Circle the complete predicate in sentence B below.

Ⓑ Some rats take care of the queen.

8. Ⓨ Ⓝ

8. Circle the word below that is spelled correctly.

humorous

humorrus

humerous

___ / 8
Total

NAME: _____   DATE: _____

Read and answer each question.

SCORE

1. Ⓨ Ⓝ

2. Ⓨ Ⓝ

3. Ⓨ Ⓝ

4. Ⓨ Ⓝ

5. Ⓨ Ⓝ

6. Ⓨ Ⓝ

7. Ⓨ Ⓝ

8. Ⓨ Ⓝ

___ / 8
Total

1. Write the missing punctuation in the sentence.

If you like weird animals look up the Dumbo octopus.

2. Write the missing punctuation in the sentence.

Its found deep in the ocean.

3. Circle the word that should be capitalized in the sentence.

It gets its name from Walt Disney's flying elephant named dumbo.

4. Underline the preposition in sentence A below.

5. Circle the possessive pronouns in sentence A below.

Ⓐ   Its fins resemble big ears on its head.

6. Underline the adjectives in sentence B below.

7. Circle the adverb in sentence B below.

Ⓑ   Those big ears help it swim quickly.

8. Circle the word below that is spelled correctly.

behaivior   behavior   behavour

NAME: _____ **DATE:** _____

DIRECTIONS Read and answer each question.

1. Write the missing punctuation in the sentence.

Do you ever wonder how goods are moved around the world

2. Write the missing punctuation in the sentence.

In 2013 a container ship set a new record for size.

3. Circle the word that should be capitalized in the sentence.

Built by a danish shipbuilder, it is one of three identical ships.

4. Underline the helping verb in sentence A below.

5. Circle the complete subject in sentence A below.

A The ship can carry 16,000 shipping containers.

6. Underline the complete predicate in sentence B below.

7. Circle the verb in sentence B below.

B The builder plans to make an even bigger ship!

8. Circle the word below that is spelled correctly.

spaccious   spaciouss   spacious

1. Ⓨ Ⓝ

2. Ⓨ Ⓝ

3. Ⓨ Ⓝ

4. Ⓨ Ⓝ

5. Ⓨ Ⓝ

6. Ⓨ Ⓝ

7. Ⓨ Ⓝ

8. Ⓨ Ⓝ

___ / 8
Total

NAME: _____ DATE: _____

DIRECTIONS Read and answer each question.

1. Ⓨ Ⓝ

2. Ⓨ Ⓝ

3. Ⓨ Ⓝ

4. Ⓨ Ⓝ

5. Ⓨ Ⓝ

6. Ⓨ Ⓝ

7. Ⓨ Ⓝ

8. Ⓨ Ⓝ

___ / 8
Total

1. Write the missing punctuation in the sentence.

If you are Irish, you may celebrate St. Patricks Day.

2. Write the missing punctuation in the sentence.

Its thought that St. Patrick drove snakes out of Ireland.

3. Circle the word that should be capitalized in the sentence.

He was actually born in cumbria, England, and taken to Ireland as a slave.

4. Underline the verbs in sentence A below.

5. Circle the pronoun in sentence A below.

Ⓐ After several years, he escaped and returned later as a missionary.

6. Underline the contraction in sentence B below.

7. Circle the proper noun in sentence B below.

Ⓑ Also, snakes didn't exist in Ireland.

8. Circle the word below that is spelled correctly.

misunderstood

misunderstod

misunderstude

NAME: _____ DATE: _____

DIRECTIONS Read and answer each question.

1. Write the missing punctuation in the sentence.

Whats a pizza without tomato sauce?

1. Ⓨ Ⓝ

2. Write the missing punctuation in the sentence.

When tomatoes were first brought to Europe they were thought to be deadly.

2. Ⓨ Ⓝ

3. Ⓨ Ⓝ

3. Circle the word that should be capitalized in the sentence.

An explorer named cortez brought seeds from Mexico to Europe.

4. Ⓨ Ⓝ

4. Underline the complete subject in sentence A below.

5. Ⓨ Ⓝ

5. Circle the verb in sentence A below.

A The plant resembled deadly nightshade, a poisonous plant.

6. Ⓨ Ⓝ

6. Underline the verbs in sentence B below.

7. Ⓨ Ⓝ

7. Circle the plural noun in sentence B below.

B Doctors also worried that too much acid was deadly.

8. Ⓨ Ⓝ

___ / 8
Total

8. Circle the word below that is spelled correctly.

cucumber

cucummber

cuccumber

NAME: _____ **DATE:** _____

DIRECTIONS Read and answer each question.

1. Ⓨ Ⓝ

1. Write the missing punctuation in the sentence.

If you want to watch crystals grow try making rock candy.

2. Ⓨ Ⓝ

2. Write the missing punctuation in the sentence.

Youll need some string, a clean jar, a pencil, a spoon, sugar, and water.

3. Ⓨ Ⓝ

3. Circle the word that should be capitalized in the sentence.

boil enough water to almost fill the jar, and stir in lots of sugar.

4. Ⓨ Ⓝ

4. Underline the adjectives in sentence A below.

5. Ⓨ Ⓝ

5. Circle the conjunction in sentence A below.

Ⓐ Tie the string on the pencil and hang it in the sugary water.

6. Ⓨ Ⓝ

6. Underline the adverb in sentence B below.

7. Ⓨ Ⓝ

7. Circle the prepositional phrase in sentence B below.

Ⓑ Sugar crystals will grow slowly on the string.

8. Ⓨ Ⓝ

___ / 8
Total

8. Circle the word below that is spelled correctly.

disolve   dissolve   dessolve

NAME: _____ **DATE:** _____

DIRECTIONS   Read and answer each question.

1. Write the missing punctuation in the sentence.

There werent many books for kids in colonial times.

1. Ⓨ Ⓝ

2. Write the missing punctuation in the sentence.

If you were lucky you got to go to school instead of work all day.

2. Ⓨ Ⓝ

3. Ⓨ Ⓝ

3. Circle the word that should be capitalized in the sentence.

The first American schoolbook was the <u>new England Primer</u>.

4. Ⓨ Ⓝ

4. Underline the conjunction in sentence A below.

5. Ⓨ Ⓝ

5. Circle the verb in sentence A below.

Ⓐ The primer included poetry, prayers, and an illustrated alphabet.

6. Ⓨ Ⓝ

6. Underline the preposition in sentence B below.

7. Ⓨ Ⓝ

7. Circle the possessive pronoun in sentence B below.

Ⓑ For many children, this was their only book.

8. Ⓨ Ⓝ

___ / 8
Total

8. Circle the word below that is spelled correctly.

ignorence

ignorance

ignoranse

NAME: _____ DATE: _____

DIRECTIONS Read and answer each question.

1. Write the missing punctuation in the sentence.

1. Ⓨ Ⓝ

Belle Boyd didnt grow up intending to be a spy.

2. Ⓨ Ⓝ

2. Write the missing punctuation in the sentence.

Union soldiers were staying at her fathers hotel.

3. Ⓨ Ⓝ

3. Circle the word that should be capitalized in the sentence.

4. Ⓨ Ⓝ

She charmed secrets from a Union soldier and passed them to confederate generals.

5. Ⓨ Ⓝ

4. Underline the helping verb in sentence A below.

6. Ⓨ Ⓝ

5. Circle the prepositional phrase in sentence A below.

Ⓐ Eventually, she was arrested and imprisoned for a month.

7. Ⓨ Ⓝ

6. Underline the pronoun in sentence B below.

8. Ⓨ Ⓝ

7. Circle the proper noun in sentence B below.

Ⓑ She later went to England and became an actress.

___ / 8
Total

8. Circle the word below that is spelled correctly.

disgiuse

disgise

disguise

NAME: _____ **DATE:** _____

DIRECTIONS Read and answer each question.

1. Write the missing punctuation in the sentence.

For most families in the early 1950s having a television was a big deal.

1. Ⓨ Ⓝ

2. Write the missing punctuation in the sentence.

The shows were in black and white and televisions didn't get great reception.

2. Ⓨ Ⓝ

3. Ⓨ Ⓝ

3. Circle the word that should be capitalized in the sentence.

Kids liked to watch *The Howdy Doody show* after school.

4. Ⓨ Ⓝ

4. Underline the complete subject in sentence A below.

5. Ⓨ Ⓝ

5. Circle the verb in sentence A below.

Ⓐ Many families watched TV together.

6. Ⓨ Ⓝ

6. Underline the article in sentence B below.

7. Ⓨ Ⓝ

7. Circle the conjunction in sentence B below.

Ⓑ Everyone watched the same show because they had just one TV.

8. Ⓨ Ⓝ

8. Circle the word below that is spelled correctly.

electronic

ellectronic

electronnic

___ / 8
Total

NAME: _____ DATE: _____

DIRECTIONS Read and answer each question.

1. Ⓨ Ⓝ

1. Write the missing punctuation in the sentence.

Do you like to swim, hike read, or play games in the summer?

2. Ⓨ Ⓝ

2. Write the missing punctuation in the sentence.

Some kids think its fun to get a job.

3. Ⓨ Ⓝ

3. Circle the word that should be capitalized in the sentence.

You can take a babysitting course from the American Red cross at age 11.

4. Ⓨ Ⓝ

4. Underline the possessive pronoun in sentence A below.

5. Ⓨ Ⓝ

5. Circle the verb in sentence A below.

🅐 Perhaps your neighbor needs a dog walker.

6. Ⓨ Ⓝ

6. Underline the conjunction in sentence B below.

7. Ⓨ Ⓝ

7. Circle the complete predicate in sentence B below.

8. Ⓨ Ⓝ

🅑 You could also wash cars or do yard work.

___ / 8
Total

8. Circle the word below that is spelled correctly.

opporrtunity

oportunity

opportunity

 #51170—180 Days of Language

NAME: _____ **DATE:** _____

DIRECTIONS Read and answer each question.

1. Write the missing punctuation in the sentence.

Do you have a collection such as coins rocks, or stamps?

2. Write the missing punctuation in the sentence.

Its fun to see how many different stamps you can collect.

3. Circle the word that should be capitalized in the sentence.

You can get all kinds of stamps at any U.S. Post office.

4. Underline the adjective in sentence A below.

5. Circle the pronouns in sentence A below.

A You can also ask friends to give you interesting stamps.

6. Underline the article in sentence B below.

7. Circle the preposition in sentence B below.

B You can even trade stamps at a stamp club.

8. Circle the word below that is spelled correctly.

posttage

postege

postage

1. Ⓨ Ⓝ

2. Ⓨ Ⓝ

3. Ⓨ Ⓝ

4. Ⓨ Ⓝ

5. Ⓨ Ⓝ

6. Ⓨ Ⓝ

7. Ⓨ Ⓝ

8. Ⓨ Ⓝ

___ / 8
Total

NAME: _____ DATE: _____

SCORE

DIRECTIONS Read and answer each question.

1. Ⓨ Ⓝ

1. Write the missing punctuation in the sentence.

If you want to learn a challenging game try chess.

2. Ⓨ Ⓝ

2. Write the missing punctuation in the sentence.

People play chess around the world and it has even been played in outer space!

3. Ⓨ Ⓝ

3. Circle the word that should be capitalized in the sentence.

The first chessboard with light and dark squares was made in europe in 1090.

4. Ⓨ Ⓝ

4. Underline the verb in sentence A below.

5. Ⓨ Ⓝ

5. Circle the complete subject in sentence A below.

6. Ⓨ Ⓝ

Ⓐ Some schools have chess clubs for students.

6. Underline the preposition in sentence B below.

7. Ⓨ Ⓝ

7. Circle the complete subject in sentence B below.

8. Ⓨ Ⓝ

Ⓑ Chess is a game for all ages.

___ / 8
Total

8. Circle the word below that is spelled correctly.

instruction

instructoin

instructoin

NAME: _____ **DATE:** _____

| | | SCORE |

DIRECTIONS Read and answer each question.

1. Write the missing punctuation in the sentence.

If you are in South Dakota be sure to stop at Mount Rushmore.

1. Ⓨ Ⓝ

2. Write the missing punctuation in the sentence.

George Washington, Thomas Jefferson Theodore Roosevelt, and Abraham Lincoln were carved into the mountain.

2. Ⓨ Ⓝ

3. Ⓨ Ⓝ

3. Circle the word that should be capitalized in the sentence.

The man with the big idea was Doane robinson.

4. Ⓨ Ⓝ

4. Underline the pronoun in sentence A below.

5. Ⓨ Ⓝ

5. Circle the proper noun in sentence A below.

Ⓐ He wanted to bring visitors to South Dakota.

6. Ⓨ Ⓝ

7. Ⓨ Ⓝ

6. Underline the verb in sentence B below.

7. Circle the adverb in sentence B below.

8. Ⓨ Ⓝ

Ⓑ It cost nearly $1,000,000 to build.

___ / 8
Total

8. Circle the word below that is spelled correctly.

successfull

successful

sucessful

NAME: _____ **DATE:** _____

SCORE

DIRECTIONS Read and answer each question.

1. (Y)(N)

1. Write the missing punctuation in the sentence.

For hundreds of years, people didnt think the brain was that important.

2. (Y)(N)

2. Write the missing punctuation in the sentence.

If they thought about it at all, they believed that ones heart did the thinking.

3. (Y)(N)

3. Circle the word that should be capitalized in the sentence.

In egypt, the brain was scooped out through the nose before burial.

4. (Y)(N)

5. (Y)(N)

4. Underline the verb in sentence A below.

5. Circle the plural noun in sentence A below.

6. (Y)(N)

A Now, scientists know the importance of the brain.

7. (Y)(N)

6. Underline the plural pronoun in sentence B below.

7. Circle the verbs in sentence B below.

8. (Y)(N)

B They also know that there is a lot more to learn about the brain.

___ / 8
Total

8. Circle the word below that is spelled correctly.

inteligence

intelligence

intelligense

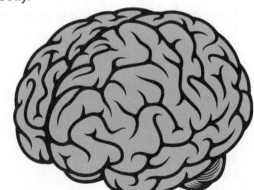

#51170—180 Days of Language
© Shell Education

NAME: _____ DATE: _____

DIRECTIONS Read and answer each question.

1. Write the missing punctuation in the sentence.

Maybe you have said, "Its raining cats and dogs."

1. Ⓨ Ⓝ

2. Write the missing punctuation in the sentence.

Youve probably never said that it is raining frogs.

2. Ⓨ Ⓝ

3. Ⓨ Ⓝ

3. Circle the word that should be capitalized in the sentence.

Yet tiny frogs have rained down in such places as bromley, England.

4. Ⓨ Ⓝ

4. Underline the helping verb in sentence A below.

5. Ⓨ Ⓝ

5. Circle the plural noun in sentence A below.

6. Ⓨ Ⓝ

Ⓐ Scientists think they were picked up and dropped by a water spout.

6. Underline the plural noun in sentence B below.

7. Ⓨ Ⓝ

7. Circle the contraction in sentence B below.

8. Ⓨ Ⓝ

Ⓑ You'd want a strong umbrella in a rain of frogs!

___ / 8
Total

8. Circle the word below that is spelled correctly.

astonishmeant

astonishment

astonishmentt

ANSWER KEY

Day 1
1. America's first spy went to work during the Revolutionary War.
2. He was a teacher until the war broke out, and then he joined the militia.
3. Nathan Hale disguised himself as a **Dutch** teacher.
4. The, his, true
5. discovered
6. British
7. the
8. intelligent

Day 2
1. "Ouch! I just got scratched by a thorn," Marnie said.
2. "Actually, those aren't really thorns," Pedro pointed out.
3. Marnie and Pedro were at the Municipal **Gardens**.
4. if
5. Marnie
6. are
7. prickles
8. cautious

Day 3
1. Edgar Degas, born in 1834, became a famous painter.
2. During his early years of painting, he wanted to be a history painter.
3. He practiced by painting in a museum called the **Louvre**.
4. very
5. dancers
6. see
7. his
8. magnificent

Day 4
1. J. Patrick Lewis once saw a white rainbow.
2. Also known as a fog bow, it inspired Lewis.
3. He wrote his first children's book, **A Russian Folktale**.
4. his
5. publishers, years
6. Monumental Verses
7. has
8. excellence

Day 5
1. If he really existed, Robin Hood lived in the year 1225.
2. One man, a robbery suspect, had a name similar to Robin Hood.
3. This man lived near Sherwood **Forest**, in England
4. He
5. and
6. can't
7. Robin Hood
8. devious

Day 6
1. More than 100 years ago, on a dark night, a writer stared at Mars.
2. As he looked through a telescope, H. G. Wells thought about Mars.
3. His thoughts led him to write the book **The** War of the Worlds.
4. this, a, Martian, the
5. was
6. the
7. and
8. anxious

Day 7
1. Do you watch television shows about hospitals or crime?
2. A lot of what you see, such as blood and injuries, is fake.
3. Michael **Crichton**, a writer and a TV producer, went to medical school.
4. his
5. stories
6. wrote, pay
7. He
8. guidance

Day 8
1. Years ago, people used cowrie shells, cacao beans, and wheat for money.
2. Wampum, which was exchanged by American Indians, was made of polished beads from shells.
3. The **Aztecs** in Central Mexico used cacao beans when shopping.
4. Cacao beans
5. were
6. if
7. your
8. preferred

Day 9
1. If you think climbing walls is a new idea, you'd be wrong.
2. In 1939 , Clark Schurman made the first wall climb in Seattle, Washington.
3. Clark Schurman was a **Boy Scout** leader who loved climbing.
4. the
5. He
6. After his death
7. was
8. equipment

Day 10
1. In 1955, Maurice Sendak was working on a children's book.
2. At first, he called the book Where the Wild Horses Are.
3. Then he tried Where the Wild Animals **Are**.
4. he
5. Finally
6. was
7. on
8. mischief

Day 11
1. The Tower of London, with its huge walls, is more than a tower.
2. In the 1070s, William the Conqueror started building the fortress.
3. It was built on the **Thames**, a river, and looks a lot like a castle.
4. took
5. Kings and queens
6. Sometimes
7. they
8. centuries

Day 12
1. Sometimes we worry about big things, and sometimes we worry about small things.
2. Doctors, as it happens, worry about some of the trillions of microbes in your body.
3. One virus, named after the **Ebola** River, caused hundreds of deaths in 1976.
4. closely
5. Scientists
6. made
7. In 2014, of the disease
8. occurrence

ANSWER KEY (cont.)

Day 13
1. Do you do "the wave" at football games?
2. The wave was first seen on television on October 15, 1981.
3. George Henderson, a big fan, first started it at San Jose State **University**.
4. had, stand, cheer
5. Henderson
6. a
7. It
8. joyous

Day 14
1. What did you toss in today's garbage?
2. Did you throw away paper, food, or a plastic bottle?
3. Dr. **William** I. Rathje digs through garbage that is decades old.
4. His
5. and
6. easily
7. Christmas
8. regrettable

Day 15
1. Have you heard the story about the vanishing hitchhiker?
2. Stories like these can be scary, funny, or hard to believe.
3. Jan **Harold** Brunvand studies stories like these.
4. legends
5. They
6. come
7. usually
8. incredible

Day 16
1. Do you like to tell jokes, riddles, or puns?
2. Jamie said, "What do you call an overweight feline?"
3. Cerillo said, "**A** fat cat!"
4. are
5. These
6. and
7. in each word
8. entertainment

Day 17
1. Crazy Horse, an American Indian warrior, was a brave man.
2. He didn't want American Indians to give up their ways of life.
3. He fought bravely with Sitting **Bull** at Little Bighorn.
4. of Crazy Horse
5. His
6. soon
7. but
8. defiance

Day 18
1. Pietra said, "I just learned something about the author of Peter Pan."
2. Mrs. Lucero asked, "What did you learn, Pietra?"
3. "J. M. Barrie sometimes got writer's cramp," **Pietra** said.
4. and
5. He
6. Pietra
7. also
8. flexible

Day 19
1. If you haven't read a book by Mark Twain, you may not know about the author's name.
2. Born on November 30, 1835, Samuel Langhorne Clemens had several jobs.
3. He became a riverboat pilot on the Mississippi **River**.
4. the
5. means, was
6. the, his, pen
7. adopted
8. preference

Day 20
1. In 1865, the Central Pacific Railroad track was under construction.
2. The builders needed cheap labor, so they hired many immigrants.
3. By 1868, thousands of **Chinese** and **Irish** workers had been hired.
4. for laying track
5. The, a, new
6. They
7. laid
8. unbroken

Day 21
1. Christopher Paul Curtis didn't start out as a writer.
2. For thirteen years, he hung doors on cars on an assembly line.
3. "I can't tell you how much I hated it," **Curtis** said.
4. The Watsons Go to Birmingham—1963
5. In his spare time
6. won
7. His
8. diligent

Day 22
1. During the War of 1812, the British burned the capitol in Washington, D.C.
2. A library with 3,000 books was also destroyed.
3. Thomas Jefferson, a former United **States** president, was upset by this.
4. and
5. he
6. bought
7. Jefferson's
8. remarkable

Day 23
1. If you like nonsense rhymes, you will like Edward Lear.
2. Born in 1812, he was one of 21 children!
3. Edward lived in **London** and was often sick as a child.
4. but
5. loved, became
6. for his funny limericks
7. his, funny
8. amusement

Day 24
1. In 1856, Frank Baum was born in Chittenango, New York.
2. For years, he managed theaters and worked as an actor.
3. He had a hard time getting **The** Wonderful Wizard of Oz published.
4. wouldn't
5. mistakenly
6. finally
7. paid
8. boastful

ANSWER KEY (cont.)

Day 25
1. Do you have pennies, nickels, dimes, or quarters in your pocket?
2. In 1866, the first nickel was issued.
3. It was issued by the U. S. **Mint**.
4. wasn't
5. but
6. was
7. The
8. strengthen

Day 26
1. If you want to see the largest Tyrannosaurus rex, go to Chicago.
2. Called Sue, she is 42 feet long and 13 feet high.
3. You can usually see Sue at the Field **Museum**.
4. Sometimes
5. Sue
6. in
7. museum, city
8. discovery

Day 27
1. If Ben Franklin had gotten his way, the turkey would be the national bird.
2. Franklin thought that the bald eagle, our national bird, had bad character.
3. About 46 to 50 million turkeys are sold each year for **Thanksgiving**.
4. don't
5. but
6. The, red, a, its
7. turkey's
8. vegetable

Day 28
1. When you get on a plane, you might not worry about other flying things.
2. However, birds can be a big problem for pilots.
3. Birds such as **Canada** geese have damaged plane engines.
4. work
5. hard
6. birds
7. because
8. accident

Day 29
1. For thousands of years, people have been lifting weights.
2. Weightlifters can be seen in ancient paintings, sculptures, and drawings.
3. Soldiers in ancient **China** had to pass lifting tests.
4. People
5. and
6. from bells
7. The
8. glorious

Day 30
1. Charles Lindbergh, a pilot, was famous for his flying.
2. However, his life changed completely one day in 1932.
3. His son, **Charles** Junior, was kidnapped.
4. fascinated
5. Richard Bruno Hauptmann
6. the
7. Although found guilty
8. accuse

Day 31
1. On April 22, 1970, the first Earth Day was held.
2. Gaylord Nelson, a U.S. senator, was worried about pollution.
3. There had been a massive oil spill in **Santa** Barbara, California.
4. Senator Nelson
5. to think, about pollution
6. around the world
7. man's
8. environment

Day 32
1. There's nothing more fun than a puppy, right?
2. However, maybe owning a puppy isn't right for you.
3. In many cities, such as **Chicago**, you can help by being a foster caregiver.
4. or
5. can foster
6. a, great
7. You'll
8. adopt

Day 33
1. For many years, inventors worked on making washing machines.
2. However, it wasn't until 1874 that a good machine was made.
3. That year, **William** Blackstone gave a birthday present to his wife.
4. and
5. well
6. After
7. he
8. clothesline

Day 34
1. Do you like hip-hop, ballet, or ballroom dancing?
2. Breakdancing was popular in cities such as New York City, New York.
3. Funk-style dancing developed in **California** at about the same time.
4. styles
5. dancer
6. creative, fun
7. and
8. gracefully

Day 35
1. For three weeks each summer, about 200 racers bike through France.
2. Racers bike on flat, hilly, and mountain roads.
3. The race, called the **Tour** de France, began in 1903.
4. changes
5. The route
6. about 2,000 miles
7. The
8. kickstand

Day 36
1. People who work digs are called archaeologists, and they never know what they will find.
2. They might find rare art, gold, or even a mummy!
3. During a dig in Knossos, **Crete**, an entire palace was found!
4. The huge palace
5. The, huge
6. probably
7. lived
8. skeleton

ANSWER KEY (cont.)

Day 37
1. You can touch your fingers with your thumbs, which are sometimes called opposable thumbs.
2. Some animals, such as great apes, have opposable thumbs on both their hands and feet.
3. Others with opposable thumbs include Old **World** monkeys.
4. use
5. sometimes
6. with stones
7. Some monkeys
8. thumbnail

Day 38
1. Do you use an e-reader, a phone, or a computer for reading books?
2. By sixth grade, your backpack might weigh 20 pounds!
3. Researchers in New York **City** schools weighed lots of students' backpacks.
4. may
5. Heavy
6. use
7. for
8. textbook

Day 39
1. For four years, the president of the United States has a big job.
2. The president, also serving as the commander in chief, leads the government.
3. He works with the **Senate** and the House of Representatives.
4. by the president
5. All, new, the
6. may
7. He or she
8. vetoes

Day 40
1. Have you ever thought about farming in the city?
2. Some teens spend their summers doing just that in Madison, Wisconsin.
3. They grow everything they need for salsa at the Darbo Community **Garden**.
4. grow
5. teens, vegetables, salsa
6. They
7. their
8. vacant

Day 41
1. Thanks to the high cost of gas, more people are buying electric cars.
2. These cars have a battery, which must be charged.
3. Many **American** drivers will buy one if it doesn't cost more.
4. must
5. Drivers
6. are
7. cars
8. reliable

Day 42
1. Many people fear snakes, such as the copperhead snake.
2. With its orange coloring and brown markings, it's easy to spot.
3. Copperhead bites are not usually fatal, according to **Dr**. Peter Bromley.
4. its, a, small
5. can
6. Don't
7. if
8. rattlesnake

Day 43
1. Most of us recycle paper, but do you think about tissue when you sneeze?
2. Of course, you don't want to pass along a cold with that tissue.
3. People in the United **States** use more tissues than they do in other countries.
4. from
5. tissues, trees
6. recycled
7. You
8. handkerchief

Day 44
1. When you have a birthday, do you get a swat or a pinch for each year?
2. Birthday customs, such as giving bumps and thumps, vary around the world.
3. Kids in **Brazil** get an earlobe pulled for each year.
4. Puerto Rico
5. Kids
6. are
7. and
8. occasion

Day 45
1. You'd be wrong if you think toilets are a recent invention.
2. Almost 3,000 years ago, King Minos had a flushing toilet in Crete.
3. A toilet was also found in the tomb of an ancient **Chinese** king.
4. in
5. in the city
6. the
7. By the 1800s
8. plumber

Day 46
1. What's the right thing to do when you are about to cough?
2. If you don't have a tissue, do you cover your mouth with your hands?
3. If you used to watch *Sesame Street*, you know what to do.
4. can
5. for
6. Sneeze, cough
7. or
8. prescription

Day 47
1. Would you like to know what is going to happen in your future?
2. For thousands of years, people have studied the sky for clues about the future.
3. The word *horoscope* comes from **Greek** words meaning "a look at the hours."
4. you
5. don't
6. your
7. you
8. prediction

Day 48
1. For many years, you could see ghost ships in California.
2. Rusting U.S. Navy ships, tied together, floated in a bay near San Francisco.
3. The ships, called the *ghost fleet*, were used during **World** War II.
4. were
5. Suisun Bay
6. of
7. are
8. buoyant

ANSWER KEY (cont.)

Day 49
1. Most people, when there is an emergency, dial 911.
2. It's comforting to know that help is on the way.
3. An emergency medical technician, called an **EMT**, will help.
4. directly
5. He or she
6. study, save
7. hard
8. ambulance

Day 50
1. Sarah Winchester, who inherited a fortune, believed in ghosts.
2. By 1862, she was depressed from the deaths of her daughter and husband.
3. She decided to build a house in San **José**, California.
4. if
5. she'd
6. Winchester Mystery House
7. is
8. basement

Day 51
1. In 1929, no one realized just how bad times were going to get.
2. Many banks failed, and people lost all their savings.
3. The **Great** Depression lasted more than ten years.
4. People
5. struggled to find jobs of any kind
6. slowly
7. New, the, the
8. hardship

Day 52
1. Do you know how much a cup of gold, if flattened, could cover?
2. That gold, when flattened very thin, could cover a football field.
3. Experts think that only about 10 percent of the gold in **California** has been found.
4. would
5. A, a
6. down
7. and
8. precious

Day 53
1. If you live in the northern states, it probably snows in the winter.
2. What's it like to have more than 100 inches of snow each winter?
3. People in **Juneau**, Alaska, have about that much snow every year.
4. Canada
5. call
6. call
7. watery
8. measure

Day 54
1. During World War II, some men in Norway wanted to smuggle gold past the Nazis to a ship.
2. Young Peter overhears his uncle talking to them, and Peter gets an idea.
3. Peter tells **Uncle** Victor that he and his friends can sneak the gold to the ship.
4. zip
5. The children
6. <u>Snow Treasure</u>
7. You
8. invisible

Day 55
1. Do you believe in sea monsters?
2. If you saw a giant squid, you'd believe sea monsters exist.
3. This sea monster's name is **Architeuthis**.
4. is
5. This, giant, a, school
6. Its
7. are
8. tentacles

Day 56
1. Do you know what the words *taw, aggie,* and *mibs* mean?
2. If you do, you probably play marbles.
3. Marbles have been found in the tombs of ancient **Egyptians**.
4. is
5. aggie, marble, stone, agate
6. different
7. and
8. hopscotch

Day 57
1. Do you do ten, twenty, or thirty minutes of homework each night?
2. If you are in fifth grade, you might be expected to do fifty minutes.
3. In the United **States**, many students do about ten minutes per grade.
4. a
5. in a quiet place
6. you
7. short, a, big
8. assignment

Day 58
1. Some people like to combine hiking, rock climbing, and swimming.
2. Called canyoneering, it's an extreme sport.
3. A flash flood killed 21 people while they were canyoneering in **Switzerland** in 1997.
4. quickly
5. can
6. by
7. by high walls
8. tragedy

Day 59
1. Meet Nelly Bly, a famous reporter who would do anything for a story.
2. In 1887, she pretends to be crazy.
3. She is sent to Bellevue **Hospital** for the insane.
4. rescued
5. she's
6. the
7. her, she
8. journalist

Day 60
1. During the Great Depression, people moved as they looked for work.
2. Many were from Oklahoma, Texas, Arkansas, and Missouri.
3. Families could pay $1 per week to live at Weedpatch **Camp** in California.
4. Leo B. Hart
5. for the children
6. while
7. their
8. honorable

ANSWER KEY *(cont.)*

Day 61
1. Many writers, such as Scott O'Dell**,** may take nearly a year to write a book.
2. O'Dell, who did research for several months**,** then wrote for another six months.
3. He received the **Newbery** Medal for Island of the Blue Dolphins.
4. O'Dell
5. for children
6. children
7. He
8. optimism

Day 62
1. Sojourner Truth's birth name was Isabella Baumfree.
2. Born in 1797**,** she was part of a slave family in upstate New York.
3. Her second master, John **Neely**, punished her often.
4. and
5. she
6. with
7. shows
8. meaningful

Day 63
1. The first president, George Washington**,** loved ice cream.
2. In May 1784**,** he got a machine for making ice cream.
3. Mrs. **Martha** Washington served ice cream at her parties.
4. Mount Vernon
5. his
6. spent
7. Washington
8. enjoyment

Day 64
1. In 1940**,** everyone thought that the only cartoonists were men.
2. However**,** one was actually a woman.
3. Instead of using her real name, **Dalia** Messick changed her name to Dale.
4. Brenda Starr
5. a, glamorous
6. and
7. were
8. acceptable

Day 65
1. When the United States had its 100th birthday**,** it got a big present.
2. The people of France**,** wanting to help celebrate, sent us the Statue of Liberty.
3. France had helped the country during the American **Revolution**.
4. The statue
5. came
6. was
7. and
8. independence

Day 66
1. Tatanka-Iyotanka, who lived from 1831 to 1890**,** was a Hunkpapa Lakota chief.
2. Known as Sitting Bull**,** he was very courageous.
3. Gold was discovered in the Black **Hills**, a sacred area to many tribes.
4. and
5. Sitting Bull, Crazy Horse
6. They
7. defeated, led
8. rebellious

Day 67
1. Leo Lionni was born in Amsterdam, Holland.
2. After coming to the United States in 1931**,** he started a career in graphic design.
3. You may have heard of some of his books, such as Swimmy or **Frederick**.
4. his
5. He
6. for his book illustrations
7. the
8. style

Day 68
1. Have you ever needed help with spelling**,** writing, or reading?
2. It's sometimes hard to get homework done.
3. Todd **Strasser**, a writer of many books, needed reading tutors.
4. was
5. My
6. mostly
7. Todd added
8. different

Day 69
1. Martin Luther King Jr. was born on January 15, 1929.
2. He had an older sister and a younger brother**,** so he was the middle child.
3. He grew up in Atlanta, **Georgia**.
4. and
5. a
6. is
7. His
8. tolerance

Day 70
1. Do you know how much you should exercise each week**?**
2. Experts say kids should do exercises that strengthen muscles**,** strengthen bones, and get you moving.
3. **Try** to do sixty minutes of exercise three times a week.
4. can
5. games
6. for you
7. that's
8. movement

Day 71
1. Imagine having to escape Paris, France**,** on a bicycle.
2. In 1940**,** Margret and Hans Rey took very little along when they fled the Nazis.
3. They did take their book manuscripts, including **Curious George**.
4. The, curious
5. wasn't
6. Fifi
7. was
8. trepidation

Day 72
1. "Hurry up**!** We're going to be late!" said Washington.
2. It was June 10**,** the last day of fifth grade.
3. Washington got an award for Most Improved **Reader**.
4. for him
5. Washington's
6. with pizza and lemonade
7. celebrated
8. graduation

Day 73

1. "Ouch!" Rina said.
2. "I've been bitten by a mosquito!" she exclaimed.
3. Most mosquito bites are just annoying, but some spread the West **Nile** virus.
4. That virus
5. can
6. are, stay
7. mosquitos
8. nuisance

Day 74

1. Washington, D.C., is the capital of the United States.
2. There's plenty to see and do in the capital.
3. The Smithsonian **Institution** includes many museums.
4. National Zoo
5. museums
6. in
7. statues, areas
8. monument

Day 75

1. There's an interesting thing happening in some schools in South Korea.
2. Some of the teachers are robots.
3. The robots are controlled by **English** teachers in another country.
4. see, hear
5. teachers, children
6. The, extra, the
7. but
8. attendance

Day 76

1. If you are called a Benedict Arnold, that is an insult.
2. During the Revolutionary War, Arnold was thought to be a hero.
3. However, in 1779 he decided to help the **British**.
4. and
5. Arnold
6. stands
7. for traitor
8. deceitful

Day 77

1. Do you know where the coldest, driest, and windiest place is on Earth?
2. If you said *Antarctica*, you would be correct.
3. One of the most famous polar explorers is **Roald** Amundsen.
4. the, first, the
5. was
6. He
7. strong, sled, his, the
8. continent

Day 78

1. In the early 1970s, many people began to use a new tool.
2. This small, powerful calculator fit in a pocket.
3. The **Chinese** invented a calculator, too.
4. has been used for thousands of years
5. Their
6. a
7. don't
8. accurate

Day 79

1. On November 5, 1872, several women got into a lot of trouble.
2. They'd go down in history just for trying to vote.
3. Susan B. **Anthony** led the group of women.
4. and
5. She
6. lost, paid
7. she
8. adjourn

Day 80

1. Have you ever been entertained by a mime?
2. A mime tells a story using gestures, movement, and expressions.
3. Marcel Marceau studied acting in **Paris**, France.
4. Bip
5. He
6. a, floppy, a
7. with
8. appearance

Day 81

1. One legend tells about a monster with a long neck, a bird head, and a booming voice.
2. Called a *bunyip*, it is thought to eat people when it can't find other food.
3. It is believed to live in swamps, rivers, or lakes in the **Australian** outback.
4. bunyips, people
5. in people
6. or
7. Its, evil
8. annoying

Day 82

1. Squirrels, which live in most countries, are rodents.
2. At just five inches long, it's hard to spot the African pygmy squirrel.
3. The **Indian** giant squirrel is three feet long!
4. Their four front teeth
5. Their
6. and
7. eat
8. chipmunk

Day 83

1. For many years, December 17 was a special day in ancient Rome.
2. There was a big festival, which they called *Saturnalia*.
3. It was held in honor of the god **Saturn**, whom they worshipped.
4. colorful
5. dressed
6. Rich
7. their
8. costume

Day 84

1. Some of Gary Paulsen's first jobs were a truck driver, a carpenter, and a teacher.
2. But he became famous for writing children's books.
3. Paulsen also completed the Iditarod Trail Sled Dog Race in **Alaska**.
4. writes
5. often
6. stories
7. his
8. exciting

ANSWER KEY (cont.)

Day 85
1. George de Mestral, an engineer, liked to hike with his dog.
2. One day, he noticed cockleburs stuck in his dog's fur.
3. That gave **Mr**. de Mestral an idea.
4. cockleburs
5. He
6. resulted
7. That discovery
8. accident

Day 86
1. Have you ever watched wheelchair basketball**?**
2. People in wheelchairs can do many sports, such as golf, tennis, and skiing.
3. Wheelchair athletics began with injured World **War** II veterans.
4. are
5. The
6. compete
7. Paralympics
8. accessible

Day 87
1. In 1913, thousands of children read the book <u>Pollyanna</u>.
2. Pollyanna, an orphan, has to live with her aunt.
3. Although she is rich, **Aunt** Polly is strict.
4. always
5. Pollyanna
6. a
7. and
8. optimist

Day 88
1. On June 22, 1947, it began to rain in Holt, Missouri.
2. For 42 minutes, it poured and poured!
3. The rain filled the Missouri **River**.
4. fell
5. of, in
6. for
7. for rainfall
8. umbrella

Day 89
1. During the Civil War, Clara Barton wanted to help the wounded.
2. However, women were not allowed to work in hospitals or on the battlefield.
3. She wouldn't give up and was known as the Angel of the **Battlefield**.
4. Red Cross, Europe
5. learned
6. for
7. Barton, American National Red Cross
8. sensible

Day 90
1. If you had to name a new flower, how would you choose a name?
2. Would you call it *blazing star, candytuft,* or *cowslip*?
3. Those names are all used, along with *drumstick, lobster claw,* and **Queen Anne's** *lace*.
4. Some, a
5. are
6. names
7. flower's
8. variable

Day 91
1. If you have a fever, aches, chills, and a cough, you may have the flu.
2. The word *flu* is short for *influenza,* and it can make you very sick.
3. The Centers for Disease Control and **Prevention** keep track of the flu.
4. often
5. get
6. the
7. your
8. unbearable

Day 92
1. The Bermuda Triangle has been a mysterious area for many years.
2. Legends claim that many planes, ships, and people have disappeared there.
3. It is in the western part of the Atlantic **Ocean**.
4. dangerous
5. it's
6. can be
7. for
8. impossible

Day 93
1. When the circus came to town, it was very exciting.
2. There was a parade of animals, and a band was pulled in a wagon.
3. Circus owners, such as P. T. **Barnum**, wanted to attract attention.
4. also
5. Politicians
6. you're
7. join, jumping
8. meaningful

Day 94
1. When times are hard, many people lose their homes.
2. Families may move in with relatives, or they may live in shelters.
3. Some people get help from the United **States** government.
4. or
5. their
6. The
7. hard
8. penniless

Day 95
1. Has someone ever said to you that a watched pot never boils**?**
2. You've been learning about time since you were born.
3. A researcher named Jennifer **Coull** says that time drags when we are bored.
4. happy, excited
5. we
6. something
7. quickly
8. inevitable

Day 96
1. If you were from China, it was hard to come to America after 1882.
2. By then, the Chinese Exclusion Act of 1882 limited the people who could enter from China.
3. Immigrants were held on Angel **Island** near San Francisco for weeks or more.
4. to prove, in America
5. relatives
6. were
7. Some, the, a
8. eligible

ANSWER KEY (cont.)

Day 97
1. Do you have a favorite musical group**?**
2. If you grew up in the 1960s**,** it might have been the Beatles.
3. They started out by performing in **Liverpool**, England.
4. in
5. invaded
6. for
7. Beatles, *Beatlemania*
8. faithful

Day 98
1. For more than 50 years**,** people have known about James Bond.
2. In addition to reading books**,** they have watched movies about this spy.
3. Ian **Fleming** wrote twelve novels about Bond.
4. stories, agents
5. his
6. Actors
7. have
8. apparent

Day 99
1. On November 14, 1963**,** something amazing happened.
2. While scientists watched**,** an island was born.
3. It happened in the **North** Atlantic near Iceland.
4. and
5. An, underwater, the, brown
6. By the next night
7. was
8. unexpected

Day 100
1. Each year**,** avalanches take about 150 lives.
2. It's rare when a person survives after 15 minutes of being buried in an avalanche.
3. Rescue teams often use **German** shepherds when searching for people.
4. These dogs
5. their
6. of smell
7. They
8. predicament

Day 101
1. You might greet a friend with a high five**,** a hug, or a kiss.
2. Years ago**,** your rank determined how you kissed a person.
3. During the Middle **Ages** in Europe, you'd kiss people below you on the hand.
4. on the knee
5. You'd
6. were
7. Religious, the
8. respectable

Day 102
1. In 1963**,** there was a lot of conflict over civil rights.
2. Many businesses**,** clubs, and schools refused entry to African Americans.
3. A bomb was set off in a church in **Birmingham**, Alabama.
4. in the blast
5. were
6. The Watsons Go to Birmingham—1963
7. You
8. horrible

Day 103
1. It was a special night in Hollywood on February 29**,** 1940.
2. Hattie McDaniel, who was African American**,** won an Academy Award.
3. She won it for her role in the movie *Gone with the **Wind**.*
4. to win an Oscar
5. the, first, an
6. Hattie McDaniel, October
7. died
8. segregation

Day 104
1. In medieval Europe**,** some young men were trained to become soldiers.
2. They were trained in using weapons**,** handling horses, and appropriate behavior.
3. The code of chivalry, which is about honor, comes from the **French** word for horse—*cheval.*
4. were
5. in royal courts
6. could become wealthy
7. Successful, wealthy
8. obedience

Day 105
1. If you got married in Rome long ago**,** some practices would be similar to now.
2. You'd probably feed your spouse a piece of food.
3. During the period of the Roman **Empire**, the bride wore a wedding veil.
4. Romans
5. The, the, evil
6. on
7. on their thumbs
8. elegant

Day 106
1. For decades**,** the most valuable baseball cards were of Honus Wagner.
2. Wagner's cards were sold with cigarette packs.
3. They were issued by the American Tobacco **Company**.
4. their, he
5. Wagner
6. his
7. cards
8. distribute

Day 107
1. Have you ever really wanted a certain toy**,** pair of shoes, or game?
2. You're not the first person to follow a fad.
3. One goofy fad dates back to the 1400s in **Europe**.
4. wore
5. Men
6. were
7. and
8. curious

Day 108
1. Once you hear a group of howler monkeys**,** you'll never forget it.
2. They're so loud that you can hear them more than a mile away!
3. If you want to hear them, visit South America or **Central** America.
4. have
5. The, large
6. use
7. also
8. chorus

ANSWER KEY *(cont.)*

Day 109

1. Have you ever read stories about giant squid roaming the seas**?**
2. For ten years**,** a group of scientists have been trying to film one.
3. A team from **Japan** finally caught one on film in July 2012.
4. so
5. the
6. The, longest
7. The longest squid ever caught
8. creature

Day 110

1. Gertrude Ederle didn't learn to swim until she was nine years old.
2. But she became famous for her swimming on August 6, 1926.
3. She was the first woman to swim the English **Channel**.
4. during the swim
5. Her
6. for
7. Ederle
8. mission

Day 111

1. During the 1700s**,** dating in America was very different from how it is now.
2. People worked long hours**,** so courting waited until evening.
3. People in the **American** colonies also lived far apart, and houses were small.
4. would
5. parents, sons, daughters, suitors
6. included
7. Dates
8. discouragement

Day 112

1. Are you creative**,** hardworking, clever, and adaptable?
2. If you like taking risks**,** you might be a good entrepreneur.
3. Bill Gates, the founder of Microsoft **Corporation**, is an entrepreneur.
4. You
5. don't
6. and
7. a, good
8. brilliant

Day 113

1. If a hummingbird follows you, look closely.
2. It could be a hummingbird, or it could be a very small spy plane!
3. **There** is a tiny robot hummingbird with a camera onboard.
4. by
5. by a pilot
6. may, be
7. It
8. obedient

Day 114

1. Every day is Valentine's Day for owl monkeys.
2. Once they get together**,** a male and female stay together.
3. Found in Central America and **South** America, they have another special habit.
4. very
5. The
6. with
7. feed, carry, play
8. faithfully

Day 115

1. When you walk on the beach**,** do you search for shells?
2. A sand dollar is a round, gray shell**,** and it has a star on the back.
3. Sand dollars are called *pansy shells* in **South** Africa.
4. once
5. A
6. used its spines to dig in the sand
7. its
8. peculiar

Day 116

1. Have you ever watched a snake flick out its tongue**?**
2. That long, forked tongue is used for smelling.
3. Most snakes in the **United** States aren't poisonous.
4. have
5. snakes, heads
6. too
7. slitted
8. vicious

Day 117

1. It's a myth that cats always land on their feet.
2. However**,** they usually do, and they learn how as kittens.
3. One cat, named **Sugar**, fell 19 stories and survived!
4. during
5. during a fall
6. they
7. the
8. adjust

Day 118

1. Vampire bats feed on cows**,** pigs, and horses.
2. They'll fly out each night in search of something to bite.
3. They can be found in **Mexico** and other countries.
4. and
5. bites, laps
6. doesn't
7. The, tiny, the
8. discomfort

Day 119

1. The bald eagle isn't really bald.
2. The eagle's head is covered with white feathers.
3. The bald eagle can be found throughout **North** America.
4. comes
5. from
6. means
7. Piebald
8. symbol

Day 120

1. In 1947**,** computers were rare and complicated to use.
2. Is your computer ever affected by a virus or a "bug" in the software?
3. Computers at Harvard **University** began having problems.
4. was
5. A moth
6. carefully
7. The, computer, the
8. investigation

ANSWER KEY (cont.)

Day 121

1. According to legend, potato chips were invented by accident.
2. A customer sent back his french fries, and he said they were too soggy.
3. Annoyed, the head chef at Moon's Lake **House** Resort made thin, crisp chips.
4. The customer
5. loved
6. George Crum and his sister Katie
7. claimed
8. preference

Day 122

1. "*Who, who, who*," say many owls at night.
2. Not all owls hoot, but they all hunt.
3. Owls are found almost everywhere except **Antarctica**.
4. see and hear
5. well
6. are
7. Their
8. midnight

Day 123

1. Sea otters are well suited for swimming in cold, icy, or freezing waters.
2. Because of their fine fur, many sea otters were killed in the 1700s.
3. They almost disappeared in **Alaska** and California.
4. Sea otters and seals
5. are
6. otters
7. A, a
8. preventable

Day 124

1. Have you ever seen an ostrich?
2. It's the world's largest bird.
3. **The** ostrich also lays the largest egg.
4. eggs
5. You
6. its
7. or
8. tremendous

Day 125

1. A giraffe may have a long neck, but it doesn't have much of a voice.
2. They'll moo like cows to their babies.
3. Found in **Africa**, they may snort or grunt a bit.
4. that, long, two
5. is
6. and
7. easily
8. obvious

Day 126

1. The invention of the x-ray, which occurred in 1895, changed medicine.
2. The invention wasn't really planned.
3. Wilhelm **Conrad** Röntgen tried taking pictures with a cathode ray projector.
4. showed
5. of
6. Röntgen
7. said, stood
8. achievement

Day 127

1. Just one bit of dust can make you shout, "Achoo!"
2. Your lungs, not liking that bit of dust, force it out.
3. When you sneeze, many people say, "**Bless** you!"
4. your
5 during
6. was
7. to
8. religious

Day 128

1. It's always fun to see butterflies in the summer.
2. After coming out of hibernation, monarch butterflies look for mates.
3. By March or **April**, they are laying their eggs.
4. The eggs
5. hatch
6. By, into
7. have
8. migrate

Day 129

1. Have you noticed that fish never blink?
2. Most fish can't blink because only sharks have eyelids.
3. When asked if fish sleep, one scientist said, "**Most** fish do rest."
4. do not sleep like humans do
5. Fish
6. they're
7. to danger
8. opponent

Day 130

1. Sometimes, a plane makes a sound like thunder, "Boom!"
2. It's called a *sonic boom.*
3. Chuck **Yeager** first broke the sound barrier in 1947.
4. is
5. is a giant shock wave
6. It, your
7. house
8. physical

Day 131

1. Drivers of cars watch for stop signs, yield signs, and traffic lights.
2. In 1914, the first electric traffic lights were installed in Cleveland, Ohio.
3. They were placed at the corner of Euclid Avenue and **East** 105th Street.
4. The system
5. of red and green lights
6. were
7. traffic
8. vehicle

Day 132

1. Perhaps it's just a story, but the sandwich may have been invented by an earl.
2. In England, being an earl showed you were important.
3. John Montagu was the fourth Earl of **Sandwich**, England.
4. and
5. didn't
6. the
7. He
8. royalty

ANSWER KEY (cont.)

Day 133
1. Do you put grape, strawberry, or raspberry jelly on your toast?
2. As early as the 1600s, recipes for making jam were published in America.
3. During World **War** I, overseas soldiers were sent "grapelade."
4. they
5. After
6. and
7. is
8. devour

Day 134
1. On August 8, 1829, the first steam locomotive in America rolled down the tracks.
2. Built for hauling coal, the tracks were in Honesdale, Pennsylvania.
3. The locomotive was called the Stourbridge **Lion**.
4. The engine
5. on its front
6. locomotive
7. Smithsonian Institution
8. engineer

Day 135
1. When a giant panda is born, it isn't exactly giant.
2. Cubs, which weigh a few ounces at birth, will gain about 300 pounds.
3. Wild pandas only live in remote areas of **China**.
4. are
5. pandas
6. study
7. captive
8. disappear

Day 136
1. If you ever need help, you should know about the SOS signal.
2. The letters, coming from the dots and dashes of Morse code, don't stand for words.
3. The first use of SOS was in 1909 by wireless operators on the SS *Arapahoe*.
4. were
5. Before
6. countries
7. have
8. establish

Day 137
1. "Nighty night, sleep tight. Don't let the bedbugs bite."
2. There's a story about that rhyme.
3. **In** colonial days, people had to tighten the ropes under beds.
4. ropes
5. soundly
6. does
7. the
8. hygiene

Day 138
1. When your dentist says, "Open wide," do you think about the chair you are in?
2. In the early 1800s, dentists added features such as headrests to chairs.
3. Mr. M. **Waldo** Hanchett was granted the first patent for his dentist chair design.
4. a, an, adjustable
5. and
6. of
7. can
8. examination

Day 139
1. Do you know how ships travel between the Atlantic and Pacific oceans?
2. They can go around South America, or they can use a shortcut.
3. The shortcut is the Panama **Canal**.
4. The canal
5. is
6. A
7. hours
8. detour

Day 140
1. In the 1700s, a new amusement was invented for the cold weather.
2. A steep hill of ice was built, and sometimes it had bumps at the end.
3. People in **Russia** rode down these hills in sleds made of wood or ice.
4. inspired
5. The, a
6. you
7. about, on
8. vacation

Day 141
1. In 1819, the first steamboat built in America crossed the ocean.
2. For 24 days, the ship used the engine or its sails to cross.
3. The ship was named the US *Savannah* after its home port in Georgia.
4. by
5. Its, return
6. It
7. Long Island
8. enterprise

Day 142
1. If you thought dragons lived only in stories, you'd be wrong.
2. Of course, these dragons don't breathe fire.
3. However, Komodo dragons, found in **Indonesia**, are dangerous!
4. They
5. and
6. Its bite
7. can
8. miserable

Day 143
1. If you lived in the 1800s, you'd probably have a job.
2. Children worked in factories, mills, and the fields.
3. The National Child Labor **Committee** was formed in 1904.
4. Laws
5. were passed
6. or
7. were
8. education

Day 144
1. You may think it'd be easy to be a clown.
2. To be a good clown, you should go to clown college.
3. The Ringling Bros. Clown College is in **Venice**, Florida.
4. need to try out to get into clown college
5. You
6. that's
7. and
8. audience

ANSWER KEY *(cont.)*

Day 145
1. Have you ever run in a marathon?
2. According to legend, the word *marathon* honors a soldier.
3. Pheidippides, a Greek soldier, ran from Marathon to **Athens** without stopping.
4. Greeks
5. He
6. and
7. the, exhausted
8. tournament

Day 146
1. After 73 years underwater, the wrecked *Titanic* was found.
2. Dr. Robert Ballard led the team that found the ship.
3. A team of American and **French** researchers had searched together.
4. their
5. used
6. The ship
7. sank
8. disaster

Day 147
1. In 1905, a boy left water, powdered soda, and a stick in a cup outside.
2. It was a cold night, and the mixture froze.
3. Frank **Epperson** found it the next morning and called it the *Epsicle*.
4. for
5. Pop's
6. he, you
7. Popsicle
8. compliment

Day 148
1. "Write what you know about," many writing teachers say.
2. Roald Dahl, author of many books, often did just that.
3. While in school, the students sometimes got **Cadbury** chocolate bars to test.
4. Dahl
5. dreamed
6. Charlie and the Chocolate Factory
7. his
8. subject

Day 149
1. If you want to hold two pieces of paper together, you might use a stapler.
2. In 1841, the first patent for a stapler was issued.
3. Samuel **Slocum**, the inventor, didn't call it a stapler.
4. called
5. He, it
6. his
7. invention
8. suggestion

Day 150
1. If you grew up in the 50s, you probably shopped at a dime store.
2. Many of the items in the store cost a nickel, a dime, or a quarter.
3. Two popular five-and-dime stores were Woolworth's and Ben **Franklin**.
4. for
5. for candy and toys
6. shop for bargains at dollar stores
7. shop
8. various

Day 151
1. Bette Greene, who became a successful writer, got just average grades.
2. That didn't stop her from thinking she was a great writer.
3. One book, <u>Summer of My German **Soldier**</u>, was turned down 17 times by publishers.
4. and
5. her
6. She
7. of writing in ink
8. challenge

Day 152
1. For 25 long minutes, Nik Wallenda walked on a tightrope.
2. It's his job to walk on a tightrope, but this was special.
3. This walk was 200 feet (60 m) above Niagara **Falls**.
4. in
5. heavy
6. His grandfather
7. died
8. conquer

Day 153
1. "Everybody in my family paints—excluding possibly the dogs," said James Wyeth.
2. Born in 1946, he left school in sixth grade so he could paint more.
3. He studied with his Aunt **Carolyn** and also got advice from his father.
4. has
5. many, famous
6. hangs
7. His
8. composition

Day 154
1. "Slow and steady wins the race" is good advice.
2. For hundreds of years, people have been reading fables.
3. Jean de la Fontaine was born in **France**.
4. Fontaine
5. wrote
6. small, big
7. with
8. serious

Day 155
1. Do you have a soda, candy, or popcorn at the movies?
2. Popcorn, which has been around for a long time, can be a tasty snack.
3. Popcorn was used in Aztec **Indian** ceremonies in the 1500s.
4. Explorers
5. a
6. ate
7. Colonists
8. favorite

Day 156
1. On April 2, 1805, a great storyteller was born.
2. His father was a shoemaker, and his mother washed clothes to earn money.
3. Hans **Christian** Andersen wasn't a great student, but he liked to write.
4. He
5. and
6. the, the, modern
7. Andersen
8. marvelous

ANSWER KEY (cont.)

Day 157
1. After decades of being called a planet**,** Pluto lost that label.
2. It's now called a *dwarf planet*.
3. Pluto was discovered in 1930 at the Lowell **Observatory** in Arizona.
4. Its
5. was
6. of
7. the, a, mythological
8. suitable

Day 158
1. Venice, a city in Italy**,** is built on more than 100 islands.
2. To get around, you can ride in gondolas**,** water taxis, or water-buses.
3. Don't miss the Grand **Canal** if you visit.
4. a, winding, the
5. from the sky
6. is
7. Venice
8. picture

Day 159
1. This salamander has many names, but the funniest is snot otter.
2. It has a large, flat body**,** and it has thick folds on its sides.
3. They can be found in the eastern United **States**.
4. Snot otters
5. shallow
6. eat
7. and
8. observe

Day 160
1. If you like haunted houses**,** you should tour the Myrtles Plantation.
2. Built in 1796 in St. Francisville, Louisiana, it is said to have several ghosts.
3. The most famous ghost is **Chloe**, a former slave, who even shows up in pictures.
4. appear, ask, are, do
5. Other ghost slaves
6. plays by itself sometimes
7. plays
8. presence

Day 161
1. The first U.S. president, George Washington**,** owned ten hound dogs.
2. Some of their names were Mopsey, Tipier**,** Sweetlips, and Searcher.
3. President Franklin D. **Roosevelt** had a sense of humor when it came to dog names.
4. He, his
5. named
6. was
7. His
8. choice

Day 162
1. Since 1922**,** 3-D movies have been produced.
2. However**,** it took about 40 years for 3-D movies to get popular.
3. The Walt Disney **Company** began making 3-D movies in 1985.
4. Some movies
5. are
6. a
7. Moviegoers
8. grateful

Day 163
1. Do you know how the Liberty Bell got its crack**?**
2. The bell, made of a mix of metals**,** cracked when tested.
3. It was recast twice, and the makers in **London** thought it was fine.
4. during
5. during the Revolutionary War
6. Philadelphia
7. the, famous
8. mysterious

Day 164
1. "Eat your carrots. They're good for your eyes." your mother may say.
2. There's a story that may have helped spread that idea.
3. A **British** fighter pilot during World War II said carrots helped his night vision.
4. were
5. at
6. and
7. People
8. twilight

Day 165
1. If you sneeze when you go outside, you're not alone.
2. Scientists aren't sure why one in three people do this.
3. Even **Aristotle**, who lived more than 2,000 years ago, wondered why.
4. so
5. your
6. you
7. Scientists
8. stubborn

Day 166
1. Wouldn't you like to be treated like a queen?
2. If you were a naked mole rat**,** perhaps you'd be the queen.
3. You can see these cute rodents at the Pacific Science **Center** in Seattle.
4. Worker rats
5. Worker
6. Some, the
7. take care of the queen
8. humorous

Day 167
1. If you like weird animals**,** look up the Dumbo octopus.
2. It's found deep in the ocean.
3. It gets its name from Walt Disney's flying elephant named **Dumbo**.
4. on
5. Its, its
6. Those, big
7. quickly
8. behavior

Day 168
1. Do you ever wonder how goods are moved around the world**?**
2. In 2013**,** a container ship set a new record for size.
3. Built by a **Danish** shipbuilder, it is one of three identical ships.
4. can
5. The ship
6. plans to make an even bigger ship
7. plans
8. spacious

ANSWER KEY (cont.)

Day 169
1. If you are Irish, you may celebrate St. Patrick's Day.
2. It's thought that St. Patrick drove snakes out of Ireland.
3. He was actually born in **Cumbria**, England, and taken to Ireland as a slave.
4. escaped, returned
5. he
6. didn't
7. Ireland
8. misunderstood

Day 170
1. What's a pizza without tomato sauce?
2. When tomatoes were first brought to Europe, they were thought to be deadly.
3. An explorer named **Cortez** brought seeds from Mexico to Europe.
4. The plant
5. resembled
6. worried, was
7. Doctors
8. cucumber

Day 171
1. If you want to watch crystals grow, try making rock candy.
2. You'll need some string, a clean jar, a pencil, a spoon, sugar, and water.
3. **Boil** enough water to almost fill the jar, and stir in lots of sugar.
4. the, the, the, sugary
5. and
6. slowly
7. on the string
8. dissolve

Day 172
1. There weren't many books for kids in colonial times.
2. If you were lucky, you got to go to school instead of work all day.
3. The first American schoolbook was the **New** England Primer.
4. and
5. included
6. For
7. their
8. ignorance

Day 173
1. Belle Boyd didn't grow up intending to be a spy.
2. Union soldiers were staying at her father's hotel.
3. She charmed secrets from a Union soldier and passed them to **Confederate** generals.
4. was
5. for a month
6. She
7. England
8. disguise

Day 174
1. For most families in the early 1950s, having a television was a big deal.
2. The shows were in black and white, and televisions didn't get great reception.
3. Kids liked to watch *The Howdy Doody Show* after school.
4. Many families
5. watched
6. the
7. because
8. electronic

Day 175
1. Do you like to swim, hike, read, or play games in the summer?
2. Some kids think it's fun to get a job.
3. You can take a babysitting course from the American Red **Cross** at age 11.
4. your
5. needs
6. or
7. could also wash cars or do yard work
8. opportunity

Day 176
1. Do you have a collection such as coins, rocks, or stamps?
2. It's fun to see how many different stamps you can collect.
3. You can get all kinds of stamps at any U.S. Post **Office**.
4. interesting
5. You, you
6. a
7. at
8. postage

Day 177
1. If you want to learn a challenging game, try chess.
2. People play chess around the world, and it has even been played in outer space!
3. The first chessboard with light and dark squares was made in **Europe** in 1090.
4. have
5. Some schools
6. for
7. Chess
8. instruction

Day 178
1. If you are in South Dakota, be sure to stop at Mount Rushmore.
2. George Washington, Thomas Jefferson, Theodore Roosevelt, and Abraham Lincoln were carved into the mountain.
3. The man with the big idea was Doane **Robinson**.
4. He
5. South Dakota
6. cost
7. nearly
8. successful

Day 179
1. For hundreds of years, people didn't think the brain was that important.
2. If they thought about it at all, they believed that one's heart did the thinking.
3. In **Egypt**, the brain was scooped out through the nose before burial.
4. know
5. scientists
6. They
7. know, learn
8. intelligence

Day 180
1. Maybe you have said, "It's raining cats and dogs."
2. You've probably never said that it is raining frogs.
3. Yet tiny frogs have rained down in such places as **Bromley**, England.
4. were
5. Scientists
6. frogs
7. You'd
8. astonishment

REFERENCES CITED

Haussamen, Brock. 2014. "Some Questions and Answers About Grammar." Retrieved from http://www.ateg.org/grammar/qna.php.

Hillocks, George, Jr., and Michael W. Smith. 1991. "Grammar and Usage." In *Handbook of Research on Teaching the English Language Arts*. James Flood, Julie M. Jensen, Diane Lapp, and James R. Squire. New York: Macmillan.

Hodges, Richard E. 1991. "The Conventions of Writing." In *Handbook of Research on Teaching the English Language Arts*. James Flood, Julie M. Jensen, Diane Lapp, and James R. Squire. New York: Macmillan.

———. 2003. "Grammar and Literacy Learning." In *Handbook of Research on Teaching the English Language Arts*, 2nd ed. James Flood, Julie M. Jensen, Diane Lapp, and James R. Squire. New York: Macmillan.

Lederer, Richard. 1987. *Anguished English: An Anthology of Accidental Assaults upon Our Language.* New York: Dell.

Marzano, Robert J. 2010. "When Practice Makes Perfect. . .Sense." *Educational Leadership* 68(3): 81–83.

Truss, Lynne. 2003. *Eats, Shoots and Leaves: The Zero Tolerance Approach to Punctuation.* New York: Gotham Books.

CONTENTS OF THE DIGITAL RESOURCE CD

Teacher Resources

Resource	Filename
Diagnostic Assessment Directions	directions.pdf
Practice Page Item Analysis	pageitem.pdf pageitem.doc pageitem.xls
Student Item Analysis	studentitem.pdf studentitem.doc studentitem.xls
Standards Chart	standards.pdf

Student Resources

All of the 180 practice pages are contained in a single PDF. In order to print specific days, open the PDF and select the pages to print.

Resource	Filename
Practice Pages Day 1–Day 180	practicepages.pdf